Empire State Ghosts

Empire State Ghosts

New York Legends and Lore

E. Ashley Rooney

Schiffer Publishing Ltd

[illegible] Road, Atglen, Pennsylvania 19310

Acknowledgments

Many of us don't quite understand ghosts. In this book, I have told or retold these ghost stories, trying from my comfortable place in the twenty-first century to make sense of the past. Throughout the work, I have endeavored to be as true to historical fact as possible. The copy editing of my wonderful cousin Betsy Johnston and the proofreading by Barbara Purchia made this work that much easier. The photography of my husband, D. Peter Lund, certainly illustrates these stories, and the companionship of Judy and Joe Meichelbeck made our study of ghosts of New York City all that much more fun.

Frontispiece:
When the Empire State Building was built, it was called "eighth wonder of the world." Constructed in one year and forty-five days on a full city block, it towered over the city at 1,250 feet. In 1972, the twin World Trade Towers surpassed it. *Courtesy of D. Peter Lund*

Ouija is a registered trademark of Parker Brothers Games.
All photos by D. Peter Lund. Text by E. Ashley Rooney

Schiffer Books are available at special discounts for bulk purchases for sales promotions or premiums. Special editions, including personalized covers, corporate imprints, and excerpts can be created in large quantities for special needs. For more information contact the publisher:

Published by Schiffer Publishing Ltd.
4880 Lower Valley Road
Atglen, PA 19310
Phone: (610) 593-1777; Fax: (610) 593-2002
E-mail: Info@schifferbooks.com

For the largest selection of fine reference books on this and related subjects,
please visit our web site at **www.schifferbooks.com**
We are always looking for people to write books on new and related subjects.
If you have an idea for a book please contact us at the above address.

This book may be purchased from the publisher.
Include $5.00 for shipping.
Please try your bookstore first.
You may write for a free catalog.

In Europe, Schiffer books are distributed by
Bushwood Books
6 Marksbury Ave.
Kew Gardens
Surrey TW9 4JF England
Phone: 44 (0) 20 8392-8585; Fax: 44 (0) 20 8392-9876
E-mail: info@bushwoodbooks.co.uk
Website: www.bushwoodbooks.co.uk

Library of Congress Control Number: 2009937637

Designed by Mark David Bowyer
Type set in Rosemary Roman / New Baskerville BT

ISBN: 978-0-7643-3418-4
Printed in China

Contents

From ghosties and ghoulies

And long-legged beasties

And things that go bump in the night,

Good Lord Preserve us!

Introduction

New York State

> A million people – manners free and superb – open voices – hospitality – the most courageous and friendly young men,
> City of hurried and sparkling waters!
> City of spires and masts!
> City nested in bays! My city!
>
> – Walt Whitman, "Mannahatta"

The Algonquin, Iroquois, and Lenape Native American groups inhabited the area when Dutch and French settlers moved into the region later known as New York in the early seventeenth century. In 1524, an Italian explorer, Giovanni da Verrazano, had sailed into New York Harbor; later, Samuel de Champlain, a French explorer, explored the upper region, and Henry Hudson, a British explorer under contract to the Dutch East India Company, claimed the region for the Dutch in 1609. By 1614, the region had Dutch forts at Fort Orange, near the site of the present-day capital of Albany. The Dutch colonized New York in 1624, at both Albany and on Manhattan Island. Great traders, the Dutch were much more interested in trapping and selling furs than in finding any New World gold or settling the land.

In 1626, the first governor, Peter Minuet, bought Manhattan, then called New Amsterdam, from the Native Americans for a bagful of baubles, valued at $24. For forty years, the Dutch ruled over the colony of New Netherlands, which even then was teeming with diversity. In 1664, the British sailed into the New Amsterdam harbor and demanded that Peter Stuyvesant surrender. At first, he refused, but after a week of talks he succumbed and gave up without firing a single shot. The English flag went up, and both state and city were named for the seventeenth century Duke of York, James Stuart, future James II and VII of England and Scotland. Fort Orange was renamed Albany.

Although victorious, the British governed a diverse society that was increasingly composed of different ethnic groups with many religious affiliations. Dutch, English, assorted Europeans, New Englanders on eastern Long Island, and assorted Native Americans all lived in this region of woodlands, lakes, and coastline with sheltered bays. With their insatiable appetite for territorial expansion, British colonists rapidly acquired land and established frontier communities.

During the period when New York State was a colony of Great Britain, England and France fought four wars for the control of North America. The strategic Mohawk Valley and the upper Hudson River and Lake Champlain were key battlegrounds. The French and their Native American allies frequently attacked the few farms and villages in the Mohawk Valley. Ultimately, British and American colonists fought the French and Canadians, with Native American allies, on both sides in the French and Indian War from 1754 to 1763.

In the colonial days, New York City was primarily a fur-trading port. Since the city was not based on religion like Puritan Boston, immigrants from many different cultures speaking many different languages found it to be an attractive new home, although it was an English city in an English colony. The city slowly grew as a commercial and export center. One of the original thirteen states of the Federal Union, New York declared its independence on July 9, 1776. The next year, on April 20, 1777, New York's first constitution was adopted.

Disguised as a Dutch schoolteacher, Nathan Hale was trying to gather intelligence about the British strength on Long Island, when he was captured on the night of September 21, 1776. The British hanged him the next morning on a gallows believed to have been erected near 63rd Street and First Avenue. *Courtesy of D. Peter Lund*

Many of the skirmishes and engagements of the Revolutionary War were fought on New York soil. On May 10, 1775, three weeks after the "shot heard around the world" on Lexington Green in Massachusetts, the Americans undertook their first offensive action against the British on Lake Champlain. Benedict Arnold and Ethan Allen captured Fort Ticonderoga, the fort at Crown Point, and Skenesborough (present-day Whitehall), a loyalist settlement. Just over a year before the signing of the Declaration of Independence, American forces on Lake Champlain were in complete control of a water highway that led directly into the heart of Quebec, but then the Americans lost the Battle of Long Island in August, which led to the British making New York City their operational base for the duration of the war. The Battle of Saratoga, one of the decisive battles of the war, was a turning point of the Revolution. The French, thrilled that the Americans had won that battle, entered into an alliance with the Americans. New York City, long occupied by British troops, was evacuated on November 25, 1783. At the end of the war, George Washington was sworn in as the first U.S. President on the steps of New York's Federal Hall.

The first government of New York State grew out of the Revolution. In June 1777, while the war was still going on, an election for the first governor was held. On July 9, George Clinton was declared elected, and he was inaugurated as Governor at Kingston, July 30, 1777. Albany became the capital of the state in January 1797.

In 1790, New York's population totaled 33,131. By 1797, it had become a bustling commercial center. When the War of 1812 with the British blockade of United States ports was over, New York became a dynamic center of foreign and domestic commerce. By 1815, Robert Fulton was operating steam ferries, which helped to link the boroughs. By 1825, when New York was about to celebrate its bicentennial year, Manhattan was establishing its lead in foreign and domestic trade.

Once disparaged as "Clinton's Big Ditch," the Erie Canal, which was built by immigrants, was completed in 1825. Now, settlers relocating from New England, eastern New York, and even Europe moved into the central and western part of the state. Others went on to Ohio and Michigan. Upstate farms and industries could easily ship their products to the large and growing market of New York City and beyond. By 1853, railroads crossed the state. Industry began to thrive in upstate cities, and communities grew along the canal.

In 1860, New York was the richest state with the most residents in the Union. About one-quarter of the state's population was foreign born, with the proportion being higher in New York City and Brooklyn. In mid century, the dramatic influx of immigrants from Germany and Ireland, who saw America as a land of opportunity swelled the population of the state's cities. Some settled in New York City; others proceeded westward via the Hudson River and Erie Canal or the railroads. By the end of the century, more Jews and Italians immigrated, often settling in New York City.

The tenement houses that housed much of the urban population were built amongst unpaved streets filled with potholes, sewage, and garbage. Horses and free-roaming pigs also contributed to the filth. Disease was rampant and spread easily amongst the closely packed citizens. The widespread use of coal coated cities in soot and polluted the atmosphere. The increased efficiency of industrial production, combined with the number of immigrants who could do the more difficult or dirty work created an expanded upper class that was now able to spend time on more recreational activities. During the 1800s, the upper classes began to migrate to the undeveloped parts of the city along railway lines, eventually creating residential suburbs and summer communities in the Adirondacks, Lower Hudson Valley, and Long Island.

In response to Lincoln's call for volunteers as the Civil War loomed, German and Irish immigrants joined New York regiments. Ultimately, nearly 450,000 New Yorkers entered the Union Army – the largest group sent by any single state. As the war intensified, the Union began conscripting men. The Conscription Act of 1863 made it possible to avoid joining up by paying $300. New York City was overwhelmed by a four-day civilian upheaval in the Draft Riots of 1863.

Despite the horror of the war, New York State grew wealthy. New York City was the focal point of supplies for the northern army. Many goods were made in the state and shipped through the state. During this time, New York City also became the publishing center for the country. After the war, industry exploded, investors made and lost fortunes overnight, and pioneers ventured throughout the United States. As the nineteenth century approached its end, architects were designing multi-storied buildings constructed on iron frames.

The Chrysler Building, an Art Deco skyscraper, is located at the intersection of 42nd Street and Lexington Avenue. At 1,047 feet, it was the world's tallest building until the Empire State Building eclipsed it in 1931. In 2007, the American Institute of Architects ranked it ninth on the List of America's Favorite Architecture. *Courtesy of D. Peter Lund*

Around 1874, Calvert Vaux designed a two-story boathouse at the eastern end of the lake in Central Park between 74th and 75th streets. In 1954, the Loeb Boathouse took its place. *Courtesy of D. Peter Lund*

In 1883, the Brooklyn Bridge linked Manhattan and Brooklyn, and by 1898, Staten Island, Queens, Brooklyn, and the Bronx became boroughs of greater New York City.

In the early 1890s, the federal government decided to assume control of immigration policy. A little island in the shadow of the Statue of Liberty became the doorway of dreams. During the beginning of the twentieth century, newcomers with hard-to-pronounce names and different cultures began to transform the nation's cities and threaten America's image of itself as an Anglo-Saxon, Protestant nation.

Although many think of New York City when thinking of New York State, the farmland, forests, rivers, mountains, and lakes dominate the state. New York's Adirondack Park is the largest state park in the United States. It is larger than the Yellowstone, Yosemite, Grand Canyon, Glacier, and Olympic National Parks combined. In 1885, New York established the first state park in the United States at Niagara Falls. The Barge Canal replaced the Erie Canal in 1918, and the system of waterways was further expanded by the construction of the St. Lawrence Seaway, which opened to navigation in 1959.

The "swords into plowshares" quotation (Isaiah 2:4) is carved on the "Isaiah Wall" of Ralph Bunche Park across the street from the United Nations. *Courtesy of D. Peter Lund*

By the twentieth century, new ideas about nationalism, expansion, and human rights were sweeping the country. The sons of immigrants now wanted nice white houses on large green grass plots. Now that the railroad was part of American life, men could travel to their jobs in the city, while raising their families in the clean country air far away from the city's harmful influence.

New York City is the headquarters for the United Nations. The facility was built in 1949 and 1950 beside the East River. *Courtesy of D. Peter Lund*

During the last century, New York City developed its premier status as a financial, cultural, transportation, and manufacturing center. It is the leading center of banking, finance, and communication in the United States and the location of the New York Stock Exchange, the largest stock exchange in the world by dollar volume. Broadway has come to symbolize live theater entertainment throughout the world. The state also has a large manufacturing sector that includes printing and the production of garments, furs, railroad equipment, and bus line vehicles. Many of these industries are concentrated in upstate regions. The city remains the nation's corporate headquarters, although one-third of the firms operate from offices outside the center city. A major agricultural force, New York is the nation's second largest wine producer by volume.

New York City offers great possibilities. There, the world comes together with neon lights, crowds of tourists, music, hopes, and dreams. *Courtesy of D. Peter Lund*

In 1886, The French gave the United States the Statue of Liberty to mark the Centennial of the American Declaration of Independence. It is often one of the first glimpses of the United States for millions of immigrants. The major ancestry groups in the state are African American, Hispanic, Italian, Irish, and German. According to a 2004 estimate, 20.4 percent of the population is foreign-born. Immigration that barely affects upstate continues to reshape New York City, which is home to more than two-fifths of the state's population. Suitably enough, the headquarters of the United Nations is in the city. Like any large urban area, New York has its problems. It also is one of the most dynamic exciting cities in the world.

"New York is the biggest collection of villages in the world."
– Alistair Cooke

"This land is your land, this land is my land, from California to the New York Island. From the redwood forest to the Gulf Stream's waters. This land was made for you and me."
– Woody Guthrie

"New York is to the nation what the white spire is to the village – the visible symbol of aspiration and faith, the white plume saying the way is up!
– E.B. White

"…the City of New York, the noblest of the American symbols."
– James Morris, Coast to Coast

"If you're not in New York, you're camping out."
– Thomas Dewey

"Give my regards to Broadway,
Remember me to Herald Square.
Tell all the gang at Forty-second Street
That I will soon be there."
– George Cohen, "Give My Regards to Broadway"

"In Boston they ask: How much does he know? In New York: How much is he worth? In Philadelphia: Who were his parents?"
– Mark Twain

"The renowned and ancient city of Gotham."
– Washington Irving

"It was a cruel city, but it was a lively one, a savage city, yet it had such tenderness; a bitter, harsh and violent catacomb of stone and steel and tunneled rock, slashed savagely with light, and roaring, fighting a constant ceaseless warfare of men and machinery…"
– Thomas Wolfe, *Of Time and the River*

"They say life's what happens when you're busy making other plans. But sometimes in New York, life is what happens when you're waiting for a table."
– Sarah Jessica Parker

WAIT FOR GREEN LIGHT
1042

GHOSTS

Throughout history, people have talked about, told stories about, and written about ghosts. Some say they have even photographed and filmed the souls of departed ones.

Certainly, many of us have had the hair at the nape of our neck prickle uneasily when we heard the creak of a stair or felt a sudden chill in the room. There are even some reports of ghosts who have been around for more than a century.

Some think that those who suffer a violent death tend to lurk near their place of death hoping to see justice done instead of departing this world. A few people even believe that these beings are trying to communicate to us through odd noises and fleeting visions.

Of course, many others deny the possibility of spirits from the past or say they are just a product of fervid imaginations. Perhaps we should try to find some answers, but meanwhile we can enjoy the stories.

Opposite Page:
Washington Square Park is one of the most famous of New York City's 1,700 public parks and a landmark in the Manhattan neighborhood of Greenwich Village. Erected in 1889 to celebrate the centennial of George Washington's inauguration, McKim Mead & White's original design for the Washington Square Arch was inspired by Roman triumphal arches. The temporary plaster and wood arch was so popular that it was rebuilt in Tuckahoe marble in 1891. In 1918, two statues of George Washington were added. The inscription on the arch reads: "Let us raise a standard to which the wise and the honest can repair. The event is in the hand of God." – Washington. *Courtesy of D. Peter Lund*

The Laird of Inverawe

The French military built Fort Carillon, later known as Fort Ticonderoga, between 1755 and 1759. The fort controlled a portage between Lake Champlain and Lake George that was strategically important during the eighteenth-century colonial conflicts between Great Britain and France. At stake were commonly used trade routes between the English-controlled Hudson River Valley and the French-controlled Saint Lawrence River Valley. The first American victory of the Revolutionary War was when Ethan Allen, Benedict Arnold, and the Green Mountain Boys crossed Lake Champlain from Vermont in 1775 and captured the sleeping British garrison at the fort. Control of the fort went back and forth until the surrender of the British army at Saratoga. Today, the restored Fort Ticonderoga is operating as a National Historic Landmark.

"I'll tell it to you as they told it to me
By the glow of the campfire burning.
By the banks of the water where we sported and played,
They once faced the fury of battle.
And up through the Champlain came the Highland Brigade
The pipes and the drummer played 'Scotland the Brave.
But when they sailed home the piper's refrain was
Oh, how cruel the volley."

– Rich Nardin, "The Piper's Refrain"

Even in August, the hall of the ancient castle of Inverawe, home of the Campbells, was chilly. The thick stone walls shut out the warmth of the day and so a great fire crackled in the hearth. In front of the massive stone fireplace slept several dogs. Musing on life on the western shore of Scotland late one evening in the eighteenth century, the laird, Duncan Campbell sat alone in the vast drafty hall, sipping a dram of whiskey. Suddenly, he heard a loud knock at the gate of his castle. The dogs began to howl as the knock became a constant thudding. Opening it, Campbell confronted an exhausted stranger, with torn and bloodied clothing.

"What do you want here?"

"Please, I have accidentally killed a man in an argument. His avengers are almost upon me. Help me!"

Feeling pity for him, Campbell promised to shelter him.

"Swear on your sword!" said the stranger.

"Whoever you have slaughtered – no matter his name or family – my sword will protect you. With my oath, I make your quarrel mine. Come in to my fireside, where I will share with you my hall. By my honor, I will see you safe from all."

He then led the stranger through the dimly lit hall to a secret room in the depths of the castle. Scarcely had he hidden the stranger when he heard men shouting and pounding at the castle gate. When he opened it, after checking that the stranger was secure in his hiding spot, two armed men stood there brandishing their weapons. "We are seeking an armed man, a bloodied murderer."

"Why did you come here?" asked Campbell.

"Because he killed your own cousin."

"My cousin!" Campbell was horrified. He now knew who the terrified stranger was, but, under the rules of the day, his earlier oath bound him to protect the murderer. Since he was also honor bound to protect his family, he was in one of those impossible moral quandaries that humans find themselves embroiled in.

That night he couldn't sleep. As he tossed in turmoil, the spectral figure of his murdered cousin visited him. The specter commanded in a dreadful voice, "Inverawe! Inverawe! Blood has been shed. Shield not the murderer!"

The next morning Campbell tried to rescind his oath, but the fugitive held him to it, "You have sworn on your dirk!"

Greatly troubled, the laird of Inverawe decided to find a way out of his predicament. He led the fugitive from the smoke-scented hall and concealed him in a cave tucked in the middle of the wild and picturesque scenery of the western Highlands near the river Awe. Feeling a sense of relief that he had shed his unpleasant burden, he returned to his castle. But once again the ghost of his cousin returned that night, declaring, "Inverawe! Inverawe! Blood has been shed. Shield not the murderer!"

The following morning Duncan Campbell again climbed to that cave, but the fugitive was gone and the cave was empty. Relieved, he returned to his castle, but his cousin's spirit came that third night. This time it sorrowfully said, *"Farewell, Inverawe. Farewell, until we meet at Ticonderoga."* Campbell had never heard of Ticonderoga, although he did wonder what the word meant.

Over the next months, his cattle sickened and died. His crops failed, and his friends shunned him. The word had gotten around that he had offered shelter to his cousin's murderer. Campbell sought to escape by joining His Majesty's 42nd Regiment of Foot, also known as the Black Watch, which was known for its Scottish determination, bravery, and valor. He rose swiftly through the ranks becoming a Major.

In America

In 1756, the British command sent the Black Watch regiment to America to fight the French. When they arrived, they learned that they were ordered to attack a large fort built near the south end of Lake Champlain in upstate New York. The French called it Fort Carillon, but its English name, "Ticonderoga," comes from an Iroquois word. Campbell shuddered when he heard the name, for it was not the first time that he'd heard it.

When they reached the fort, his fellow officers tried to disarm his fears, even telling him that they were at Fort George, not Ticonderoga, but the ghost of Donald Campbell would not let the laird escape. He came to Campbell that night, reminding him that this was Ticonderoga and that it was here that he would die. Dawn was cold and gray. A few spatters of rain blew fitfully; small patches of mists lingered in the dripping trees. On the morning of the battle, Campbell spoke angrily to his fellow officers about concealing the true name of the fort. "You have deceived me! My cousin's spirit came to my tent last night! He told me that this was the place that I would die!"

The gray light seeped bright. The flags were bright wind-driven ripples against the gray sky. The French had reinforced their fort by stacking trees in front of its thick walls. Impatient to take the fort, the British officers decided to forego an artillery attack first and commanded the Black Watch to charge. Raising their colors, playing the bagpipes, the Scots advanced. They were shouting as they moved.

"Stay tight, stay tight!" Campbell bellowed.

They could see the flame light ahead and hear the balls whistling and thumping. Shouts came from their ranks as one after another was hit. The noise was unending: gunfire, screams of the dying, and the desperate blare of trumpets. So many men had fallen that the Scots behind could not negotiate the piled bodies. Those who reached the fort were ensnared by the trees, becoming easy targets for the French sharpshooters. The battle was a disaster, ending in piles of tangled, blood-laced corpses and cripples whose cries for help were pitiful.

The Scots lost over half of their troops. Ultimately, 4,000 French defenders repelled 16,000 British troops. It was another year before the British attacked again.

From the beginning of the battle, Campbell knew that he would die at Ticonderoga. When a bullet shattered his arm, he was ready to meet his end. He was carried to Fort Edward where he died after his arm was amputated. His gravestone reads:

Here lye's [sic] the Body of Duncan Campbell of Inverawe, Esquire, Major to the old Highland Regiment, aged 55 Years, who died the 17th July, 1758, of the Wounds he received in the Attack of the Retrenchment of Ticonderoga or Carillon, on the 8th July, 1758.

Back in Scotland

Back home in Scotland, the news of the laird's death first came through the spirits. One boy who was sleeping in the same room as his father was awakened by a strange sound and a bright light. He saw a man, in full Black Watch uniform, cross over the room and stoop down over his father's bed and give him a kiss. Too frightened to speak, the boy put his head under his blanket and went to sleep. He saw the same sight again the next night. When he told his father about it, his father said, "You have seen the laird, who came to tell you himself that he had been killed in a great battle in America."

Two ladies of the Inverawe family saw a battle in the clouds, when they were crossing the bridge over the river Awe. They saw the different regimental colors and shadowy forms of soldiers in the Highland Regiment. When they heard the dreadful news from America, they discovered that the time of their vision was the same as the battle in which the head of the family fell.

Ticonderoga, New York

Author's Note: When vacationing at Saranac Lake, New York, in the 1880s, Robert Louis Stevenson listened to many tales of the Adirondacks, which became fodder for his imaginative mind. When he heard of Fort Ticonderoga's history, he published a ballad in *Scribner's Magazine* in December 1887. It became one of America's most famous ghost stories:

"This is the tale of the man Who heard a word in the night In the land of the heathery hills, In the days of the feud and the fight. By the sides of the rainy sea, Where never a stranger came, On the awful lips of the dead, He heard the outlandish name. It sang in his sleeping ears, It hummed in his waking head: The name – Ticonderoga, The utterance of the dead."

– Robert Louis Stevenson

Duncan Campbell's story also inspired Stevenson's novel, *The Master of Ballantrae*.

Ghosts of Fort Ontario

Located in Oswego, New York, Fort Ontario dates back to the mid-1700s. Oswego was once the scene of international rivalry between the French and British, and the location of one of the most important trading posts in America. Sometimes, as many as 300 traders operated out of Oswego in their own semi-permanent village of log huts, situated in the vicinity of what is now Water Street.

Britain, France, and, since 1776, the United States have occupied the fort. In 1901, it was abandoned, but when the United States army was expanded, it was revitalized. In 1946, the fort was transferred to the State of New York and developed as a State Historic Site. Today, it has been restored to depict life within the fort in 1868.

The sword and gun, drowning, fevers, alcoholism, flu epidemics, and accidents have killed over 100 individuals buried in the fort's cemetery. Its ghosts date back to the French and Indian War (1754 – 1763), Revolutionary War (1775 –1783), Civil War (1861 – 1865), and up to the last burial at the fort cemetery in 1943. Today, the restored fort is open to the public as a state historic site and was the inspiration for a famous Gordon Lightfoot song.

> "If you could read my mind love
> What a tale my thoughts could tell
> Just like an old time movie
> 'Bout a ghost from a wishing well
> In a castle dark or a fortress strong
> With chains upon my feet, you know that ghost is me
> And I will never be set free
> As long as I'm a ghost that you can't see."

– Gordon Lightfoot, "If You Can Read My Mind" (1998)

In January 1752, the garrison at Fort Ontario was running dangerously low on food and other provisions. It was so bitterly cold and so miserable that they could hardly bear to get out of bed in the morning. The snow kept coming, the wind kept howling, and the men were starving. Eight British soldiers decided to venture out of the fort's safety to visit the Indian village in the vicinity to obtain more food. Unfortunately, once they left the fort, a massive snowstorm arose. Without any shelter, they faced a nightmare of blowing and drifting snow, freezing temperatures, gusty winds, and periods of sleet. Barely able to stand upright, they wandered blindly about in the deep snow and the icy winds. As the storm worsened and the snow rose to almost four feet, some of the soldiers began to lag behind.

The lieutenant ordered a halt for the night in the dense forest. Perhaps the tall pines would protect his small force. They built a ramshackle shelter from small branches and started a fire, but it was too late for some of the group. Two soldiers died. The remaining six soldiers knew their survival depended on food and the resulting energy. Like others before them in such a predicament, they agreed to consume their dead comrades' bodies. Within days, cold winds and exhaustion felled two more soldiers. The remaining four returned to the fort with the ghosts of their fellow soldiers in their eyes.

One ghost is Corporal Fakes, an American loyalist who died from disease. His ghost, who wears the red coat, white britches, and crossed belt of a British regular, is said to have appeared to every new regiment for more than a hundred years; its appearance results in a swift decrease in the temperature in the room.

There's also Lieutenant Basil Dunbar, an officer of the 60th Foot or Royal American Regiment, who was killed in a duel at Fort Ontario in 1759. His grave is in the present Post Cemetery, and he has been seen wandering about the fort appearing dazed and confused. A third specter has been seen in a blue uniform like those worn in the Civil War.

In 1901, Fort Ontario was abandoned. Between 1903 and 1905, the post was expanded as part of the Army's reorganization. Over two dozen brick and wood frame buildings were constructed outside the old fort to house the larger number of troops and support services. The post continued to grow; by 1941, approximately 125 buildings stood at Fort Ontario.

During World War II, Fort Ontario was used as a safe haven for 1,982 refugees from war-torn Europe to await the outcome of the Second World War. In 1944, with the tide of the war becoming more positive for the Allies, President Franklin Roosevelt invited refugees who had escaped concentration camps to come to America. President Roosevelt promised Congress that the refugees would go back home when the war was over. In fact, the refugees had to sign a document to that effect.

They sailed here on a troop transport ship from the Bay of Naples. A train carried the refugees north to the decommissioned military base at Fort Ontario. They had medical care, food, school, and many of life's amenities, but they weren't free. They didn't belong legally in this country. They still were surrounded with barbed wire fences and military personnel, which must have resurrected their memories of Nazi Germany. Nonetheless, the refugees and the Oswego community began to interact. By the end of the war, in January 1946, the gates of what was now called War Refuge Center were opened. Those who wished managed to remain in America. Most likely, they left many of their own ghosts within the fort.

During recent years, paranormal investigators have recorded unusual readings and temperature drops. They have heard doors slamming, footsteps, and the laughter of children. A banging was heard once, and it was so loud that it seemed as if it was coming from every direction. In the Office Quarters Number Two, loud men's voices often awakened the investigators in the middle of the night. Ghost hunters have seen many orbs, which are commonly found in haunted areas. When they investigated, they never found anyone.

The Headless Soldier

Fort Niagara

Like many New York state forts, Fort Niagara is more than 300 years old and has belonged to France, Britain, and the United States. Since the War of 1812, Fort Niagara has served as a peaceful border post. During both World Wars, it was a barracks and training post. Today, the Old Fort Niagara Association, Inc., a not-for-profit organization, in cooperation with the New York State Office of Parks, Recreation, and Historic Preservation, run the renovated Fort Niagara State Park and museum.

The Niagara District is filled with ghosts and their stories. One of the best is about the eighteenth century French soldier who lost his head (literally!) over a beautiful Indian maiden. His killer tossed his body into the well of Fort Niagara, where it can often be seen headless today, because his head had been tossed into Lake Ontario. But let's begin at the beginning.

In 1726, the French built the four-storied fort on the south shore of Niagara River, where it flows north into Lake Ontario. The dank clammy building has little natural light; its long, dark stone hallways open into shadowy chambers on either side. No sunlight penetrates this perfect spot for ghosts. Many have reported seeing candles that are lit by unseen hands, ghostly shapes without faces, and even a ghostly German Shepherd barking at the moon. Visitors to the fort accept these occurrences as part of normal day-to-day life.

Originally, a frontier military post capable of resisting Indian attack, Fort Niagara was intended to defend France's lucrative fur trading route to the interior. During times of peace, trappers and Indians came to the fort to exchange boatloads of furs for manufactured goods. Eventually, fur traders settled their families around the fort, Indian settlements grew up in the area, and the fort served as a supply depot and trading post.

Inside the fort, the senior officers had their wives and children, but the younger soldiers were single and lonely. During peaceful times, they had little to occupy them except for petty jealousies, minor irritations, and long-controlled stress.

The northern parts of New York State are quietly beautiful. You can see shadows on the rocks, hear the wind in the trees, and the call of the Canada geese.
Courtesy of D. Peter Lund

In the 1830s, a beautiful young Iroquois woman moved into one of the Native American settlements surrounding the fort. All of the young British soldiers were most interested, but one young officer, Jacques Pepin, was particularly enamored with the lovely Kawa. Throughout the summer, when he wasn't on duty, Jacques and she happily roamed the fields carpeted in the green and gold of fresh grass, walked along the upper portion of the falls, and swam in the lake. In the evening, they would sit and listen to the whispering of the pine trees and watch the fireflies flitting through the evening's dusk. Although Kawa loved Jacques, she didn't want to leave her family, her tribe, and her country to marry a dashing French soldier who would take her back to a strange country. On the other hand, Jacques was an ambitious French soldier, who certainly didn't want to stay in the wilderness forever when he had a promising military career back in France. So, hands entwined, brows furrowed, they roamed the riverbanks debating about what to do. Then, much to Jacques' dismay, Henri LeClerc, another soldier, began to flirt with Kawa.

Jacques raged with jealousy. He was afraid of losing Kawa and angry that Henri was moving in on her. Kawa, however, was flattered. Now she had two French soldiers fighting for her attention. Their fellow soldiers were fascinated by the mounting drama. Bets were taken, rumors passed, and everyone could see the tensions mounting between the two officers.

One night both Jacques and Henri had been out drinking with friends. As they stumbled back to the fort from different directions, their paths happened to cross in the central courtyard of the fort. Recognizing his rival even in the dark of the night, Jacques drew his sword. His pent up anger at this man who was threatening his relationship with Kawa and his inebriated state surpassed any sense of judgment he might have had.

"Allez," he challenged, and Henri answered by drawing his own weapon. They advanced and retreated, cut and thrust, and counter attacked. Their blades flashed in the reflected moonlight as they slashed and thrust. Jacques forced his opponent back, step by step. Suddenly, his sword cut through flesh and bone, and Henri's head bounced along the cobbled courtyard. He had killed his fellow soldier! If he were caught, he would be court marshaled and lose his career and his love – if not his life! Jacques quickly threw Henri's head into the nearby river, where it was swept into Lake Ontario. Unfortunately, Henri's body was too heavy for him to toss into the river. He dragged it to the fort's well, removed the cover, and tossed it in.

Jacques then cleaned his sword and went to his quarters, hoping that no one would suspect him. Despite the lack of physical evidence, rumors quickly began circulating over the next couple of days that Jacques was the key to the sudden disappearance of Henri. After all, who else had a better reason to get rid of Henri? Certain that his crime was about to be discovered, Jacques knew that he should disappear. His actions had determined his decision. He would be staying in the wilderness and never have that brilliant military career. When the Iroquois packed their belongings and began the long trip back to their village a few days later, he and Kawa accompanied them.

Jacques left behind the ghost of a headless soldier who can be seen at midnight, rising out of the well, on moonlit nights, searching for his head. There's a scratching sound, a shuffling as the light disappears.

Even today, staff, visitors, and paranormal investigators confirm supernatural activity. Dancing lights dark shadows, muffled battle sounds, creaking walls, and disembodied voices are a part of Fort Niagara.

Fort Niagara
Youngstown, New York

The Ghost in the Bar

The legend of Mrs. Skene's ghost goes back to 1775 and Colonel Philip Skene.

The story begins when the British Crown, in gratitude for his services, granted Colonel Philip Skene 25,000 acres, overlooking a small village and Lake Champlain. The colonel was Royal Judge for Charlotte County and Military Governor of Fort Ticonderoga. The village of Skenesborough was named after him. Despite the important sounding positions, he doesn't seem to have made much money, because he drew on his wife Catherine's yearly dowry to help pay for the house. Perhaps that is why Catherine wrote her will to provide an annual annuity for her husband – only as long as her body remained above ground!

Certainly, the Colonel didn't want to lose his annuity so, when Catherine died, he decided to embalm her in vinegar, place her body in a lead coffin, and prop her up in a corner of the basement. That way, he was living up to the dictates of the will. Once the American Revolution broke out, and the Americans defeated General Burgoyne, Colonel Skene fled the area for Canada, leaving his wife's body in the basement to be discovered by the invading troops. They stole her rings and left her body to be found by others, who finally buried her on the property.

Some say the Americans melted her lead coffin down into bullets. Poor Catherine.

Meanwhile, Colonel Skene, who accompanied Buorgoyne's expedition, was with the British force defeated at Bennington and was captured at Saratoga. He died in England in 1810. Of course, the village named after him was renamed Whitehall.

In 1776, Congress ordered General Philip Schuyler to build a fleet of ships. Materials, supplies, carpenters, soldiers, and sailors descended upon

Skenesborough Harbor to construct the first U.S. naval fleet that summer. For this reason, Whitehall is known as the birthplace of the U.S. Navy. This fleet of thirteen ships joined the other American vessels, including the *USS Enterprise*, to form a sixteen-vessel naval fleet.

Years passed. In 1874, New York State Judge Potter and his wife, Catherine, tore down Colonel Skene's old mansion and hired Isaac H. Hobbs & Sons of Philadelphia to design an elegant, Victorian Gothic castle. Located on the side of Skene Mountain, the building was constructed from gray sandstone quarried from the mountain, with slate used in construction of the roof, dormers, and towers. The exterior included four chimneys and six dormers, and Mr. Hopson surrounded the building with fruit trees, evergreens, and flowering bushes.

The interior features three stories, each of which is 3,000 square feet in area. There are ten bedrooms, three dining rooms, and seven fireplaces. The stair railing and banister are made of mahogany, walnut, oak, and birch. Stained-glass windows are located on the stair landing and over the front door.

In 1960, a member of the new owner's family is said to have committed suicide in Judge Potter's bedroom. Visitors to that room report having feelings of dread.

Local people insist Catherine haunted the castle. They say that they have seen the ghost of a young woman dressed in a white Victorian gown and wearing an unusual ring on her left hand, walking the corridors of the manor.

The manor had many owners, but eventually it became a restaurant. Many people who enjoyed their Cosmos, martinis, and microbrews have seen Catherine frequent the bar. Maybe the colonel drove her to drink! An enterprising owner placed a coffin behind the bar in full view. He rigged the coffin to have a fake hand, wearing a ring alleged to be Catherine's. When he pulled a string, he could move the bejeweled hand. Several patrons having viewed the spindly white hand departed immediately to join AA.

Ultimately, Skene Manor was added to the National Historic Register.

In 1995, the Whitehall Skene Manor Preservation, Inc. group (also called "Save Our Skene" or 'S.O.S.") purchased the castle with the main purpose to purchase, renovate, and preserve Skene Manor for future generations.

Potter Terrace
Whitehall, New York

The Beardslee Castle Ghosts

Now a beautifully restored restaurant, Beardslee Manor, located near the town of Utica, hosts weddings and receptions. *Fodor's Restaurant Guide* says,

"Thanks to the meticulous owners, you'd never know that this 1860, Irish-style castle, now a fine American restaurant, had survived fires and years of abandonment. The place is said to be inhabited by ghosts, and that's not hard to imagine. Stone archways separate the five cozy dining rooms, where white cloths cover the tables. The food doesn't detract from the haunting ambience."

But some visitors have found that they don't have just their invited guests attending their parties at Beardslee Manor; they have ghosts too!

New York State was once a formidable wilderness. For a long time, the Indians enjoyed its great valleys and lakes, but unfortunately, the settlers' greed for land overwhelmed that desire. With their insatiable appetite for territorial expansion, British and Dutch colonists rapidly acquired land and established frontier communities. By the early sixteenth century, the French claimed most of North America west of the Appalachian Mountains. Jacques Cartier (1542) and Samuel de Champlain (1608) had established military outposts along the St. Lawrence River and into the Great Lakes, founding the territory known as New France. Trappers, traders, and Jesuit missionaries along with Indians inhabited this wilderness. From 1754 to 1763, British and American colonists fought the French and Canadians, with Native American allies on both sides in the French and Indian War.

Dark Beginnings

The Mohawk Valley was the central supply point for militia along the northern borders of the colonies. During the war, a fortified homestead, which stored munitions and powder, stood between Little Falls and St. Johnsville in the heart of Mohawk Valley. Late one night, some Indians moved stealthily into the home and into the area where the munitions were stored. Legend has it that their torches ignited the gunpowder, turning this band of Indians into a small page in history. Perhaps this is the reason that the Indians are considered the source for restless psychic energy in the area.

On the site of the old fortified house, Augustus Beardslee built a replica of an Irish castle in 1860 on a rise a few hundred feet from the highway. He had a covered walkway leading to the East Creek train station and a private semaphore installed so he could stop trains and travel to New York. In the late nineteenth century, Guy Beardslee, Augustus' son, returned from Fort Niobrara, Nebraska, with Sioux war objects, which are considered sacred by the Sioux. These Sioux artifacts, tomahawks, knives, and war bonnets, adorned the family' castle until the building burned in 1919.

Some of the Many Ghosts

The castle was partially built and owned by various people until the 1940s, when the Christensens purchased the building and turned it into a restaurant. Their happy days of innkeeping changed when Pop Christensen was diagnosed with cancer. Terminally, ill, Pop attempted suicide several times. Finally, he hung himself in the building. He may be gone, but his ghost still wanders the building in a top hat and a black suit. Occasionally, a "lady in white" joins him in his midnight forays around the castle, and a ghostly foursome periodically dines by candlelight. The castle often looks eerie because of the heavy fog drifting in from the nearby Mohawk River.

Beginning in the 1950s, strange yellow or blue lights would rush out at cars on Route 5 and even chase them down the road. The light was said to be blinding, and several fatal accidents occurred along the bend in the road where the light was seen. One survivor said, "The light rushed out from the trees and blinded my husband, who was driving." He died. Several cars have driven off the straight clear stretch of road in front of the castle.

Many report seeing a transparent figure carrying a brightly lit lantern on the roadside. Some say they have seen the ghost of Guy Beardslee roaming the grounds holding a lantern with a blue light in his hand. Several automobile accidents in this area have been blamed on him and the light from his lantern.

More recently, a couple traveling past the castle were horrified when a young lady stepped out into the road. According to the couple and witnesses in a car traveling the opposite direction, their car struck the woman. They called the police. Neither the police nor any of the parties involved could find the woman, and there were no marks on the car.

By the 1960s, young people discovered the Beardslee Family Mausoleum at the edge of Beardslee City cemetery. Late night partygoers reported seeing strange lights as well as hearing voices. Then a few people broke into the crypt and desecrated the graves. When a local person was arrested, police found Augustus Beardslee's skull in his closet. A Syracuse policeman photographed the crypt, and a strange rainbow appeared on the side of the picture, which did not follow the regular color pattern of the spectrum.

Ghost Hunters

By the 1980s, the owner of the Beardslee Manor decided to explore the truth behind all the ghost stories. He procured the services of a professional ghost hunter who spent the night and recorded whispering voices on tape in front of approximately forty reporters. Business took off as people flocked in to see the ghost. The staff did a great deal of entertaining and storytelling. The ghost hunter concluded that at least two spirits haunted the manor.

More than one psychic challenged with identifying the resident spirits has felt the presence of the woman, dressed in a white dress with a high collar and bottom sleeves. She is known as Abigail, and people believe she died the night before her wedding. Some have seen her on the grounds sitting, walking, or standing by the window. One person in particular who was unfamiliar with the property or stories of the past identified this woman further saying that she was fond of fabrics, flowers, and the castle, and that she remained here because she loved the building.

In 1984, the cathedral ceiling that had been open to the second floor was closed off, and some of the activity seemed to subside. Still footsteps are heard in the dining room after dinner service has ended; several staff members have heard disembodied unintelligible voices around them and phantom keys jingle as if someone is readying to lock up.

One night, a few staff members were playing with an Ouija board when the lights suddenly went out and a tremendous force hit one of them in the chest, pushing him across the room. People tell tales of overturned tables and chairs, silverware flying around the room, and bottles and glasses breaking when employees arrive in the morning. Three employees were chased from the building late one night by a thunderous scream or howl that surrounded them. Once the staff finished cleaning at the end of the night and had gone downstairs, nobody dared to go back upstairs alone.

The castle burned in 1989. The abandoned building became a hangout for late night parties. Those parties, the weather, and thieves destroyed it.

After three years of neglect, the castle was rebuilt and refurbished. Before the castle reopened in 1994, its owner hired a local minister to bless the castle and to keep the angry spirits at bay. The priest had some significant powers at his disposal because, since then, ghostly activity was reported to be much more subtle than in prior years.

Nevertheless, the castle has been source of many ghost stories. For some those keys still jingle; footsteps are still heard; and there's that feeling that there is something lurking there. The castle appeared in October 1999 in the *Haunted History* series on the History Channel.

---

123 Old State Road
Little Falls, New York

The Ghost of Merchant's Museum

When we think of New York City, we generally think of Wall Street, Broadway, Fifth Avenue; we think of big businesses, big apartment houses, glitter and fun. We think of well-dressed people sauntering down the avenues: the men in well-fitted suits, the women in tight skirts with high-heeled shoes. We don't think of family houses bustling with children and activity. Yet in the nineteenth century, New York City once had many family homes. The only one still preserved intact from the nineteenth century is The Merchant's Museum.

A National Historic and New York City landmark, the red brick and white marble rowhouse is the city's prime example of a Greek revival home. With its original moldings, mahogany furniture, and the family's belongings, it offers an intimate glimpse of family life during the period when New York was transformed from a colonial seaport to a thriving metropolis. Today, the house transports you back to the genteel life of wealthy New York in the nineteenth century when East 4th Street was a popular uptown address!

In 1835, Seabury Tredwell, a prosperous hardware merchant, purchased the three-year-old home for $18,000. The fifty-five-year-old Seabury, his wife and seven children moved into the house on 29 East 4th Street between the Bowery and Lafayette. The neighborhood was much more upscale than their former bustling South Street neighborhood. Just around the corner on Lafayette Place, lived many millionaires, including the Astors, Brevoorts, and the Delanos. Theaters, restaurants, and the best shops lined the streets.

Seven children make for a lively home, and then they had the eighth, Gertrude. The house bustled with activity: the crying and laughter of children, the pounding of little feet up and down the wrought iron staircase leading to the front door. The family ate many meals around the mahogany dining room table, which still remains. Eventually, beaus came calling upon Gertrude's sisters, and wedding receptions were held. Later, they mourned their dead, who lay in state in the front parlor.

Seabury had definite rules for his family. "I refuse to allow you to make a spectacle of yourself. You will live quietly by our rules."

"What do you mean, Father?" asked Julia.

"I mean that you live in this house the way we have always lived until you leave it for your own domicile. We have our own possessions, silver, china, and the like. We go to church on Sundays, do charitable work, listen to music. We have our rules, our expectations. And we don't allow our good name to be bandied about the street."

By 1870, steam trains, which had begun to replace horse-drawn streetcars and carriages, squealed on iron tracks. Telegraph wires swung overhead. The air smelled of coal fumes and wood smoke. The rich fled lower Manhattan, which had become increasingly congested, noisy, and unhealthy. People no longer lived in nearby shops and counting houses. Eventually, only three daughters, Phoebe, Julia, and Gertrude were left in the house, living on their inheritance behind the heavy red curtains and watched by the portrait of a dour-looking Seabury Tredwell.

In the nineteenth century, New York City once had many family homes.
Courtesy of D. Peter Lund

Supposedly, Gertrude wanted to leave. She told her father that she had fallen in love with a Catholic doctor, Lewis Walton. A proud Episcopalian, her father was appalled. No child of his would marry a Catholic, he thundered. They would remain true to their Episcopalian heritage. "You are a descendant of the first bishop of the Episcopal church in America. You will not deny that heritage." Gertrude wept and pled, but she was a proper Victorian daughter who knew that she had to obey her father. Seabury announced, "You must get over it. He is not a gentleman!"

Others' lives moved forward, but Gertrude had come to a halt in shades of gray as if she were living in a snapshot, frozen in place. By 1909, Gertrude was the only one left in the house, trying to keep the house "as Papa wanted." Meanwhile, the other families moved on as the theaters and shopping districts moved uptown, and factories and tenements replaced the once-splendid homes.

An odd recluse, Gertrude remained in the house until her death at age ninety-three in 1933. Many believe Gertrude's spirit remains in the house. People tell stories of sightings of a shadowy woman in a gray dress descending the staircase or hearing piano music wafting from the front parlor in the middle of the night. If you visit, you may be fortunate enough to see a teacup moving from room to room or feel a cold blast of air.

According to some, the house may well be affected by telekinetic energy. Computers have been known to freeze when the typist tries to type the name Tredwell. Paranormal investigators who have been brought in to study the house believe that the spirits in the house might be frustrated by all the changes in society.

29 East Fourth Street
New York, New York

The Haunting of Octagon House

In the middle of the nineteenth century, wealthy residents of New York City attracted by Irvington's cool summer breezes and beautiful pastoral location near the Hudson began to build large summer estates. From the late 1800s to 1920, a period often called the Gilded Age, many villages like Irvington were summer colonies for the American economic elite or the American "aristocracy" of the time. Their decisions affected American society, politics, and law. The bankers, the heads of industry, and the robber barons were the ones with the next daring idea, the next new product, and the next great invention that would help transform the country to an industrialized nation of international standing. Although the summer people often brought their servants, who were frequently new immigrants, they also employed the local people during their stay. The villagers worked in the gardens, the greenhouses, and the farms, foregoing their usual hardscrabble existence for the summer months.

One of the most unique homes built during this era was the Armour-Stiner (Octagon) House, which is the only known residence constructed in the eight-sided, slate-roofed shape of a classic Roman Temple. Five stories high, the house culminates in a many-windowed cupola. The original owner, banker Paul Armour, established the eight-sided footprint.

In 1872, Joseph Stiner, a prominent New York City importer of Chinese teas, purchased the estate, adding the dome and the veranda. He made some design changes based on his travels in China. As a result, the elaborately designed wrought iron has floral detailing and the pillars rise to flowered capitals painted in shades of rose, blue, violet, and red. The interior has painted and stenciled ceilings, gold, silver, and bronze leaf trim, and unusual eight-sided motifs. Wood paneling covers the circular room inside the dome. A spiral staircase leads to the octagonal observatory, which provides 360-degree views of the Hudson Valley.

A shrewd French widow bought the Octagon House from its former owner. The widow had a beautiful daughter called Genevieve, who had great charm, a lively temperament, black hair, and even-blacker eyes. Her mother knew that her livelihood depended on Genevieve finding a man of great wealth who would take care of them both. If her daughter married well, she wouldn't have to worry about her future.

On a nearby estate lived an American family, whose English ancestors had made their fortune in sugar. They had planned that their eldest son, William, would marry the daughter of a nearby family who would increase their family's wealth and connections. When William met Genevieve at a party, however, he fell desperately in love with the enchanting young French woman. He thought her haunting eyes were lit with intelligence, and her shape delightfully feminine.

"Do you play croquet?" William asked. "They have a game tomorrow."

"I do."

"Perhaps, I will see you there."

"Perhaps."

The next morning, a breeze blew steadily from the hills. Canopies of white clouds threw cool shadows over the croquet court, where many people were playing. William found himself looking for Genevieve and ignoring his friends. Half way through the course, Genevieve knocked her ball into the woods, murmured her excuses, and disappeared after the ball. William went after her. He found her in a rocky glen, sitting on a large fallen tree. Her hair was in curly disorder around her slender neck. He sat down beside her.

A bird trilled a long high note. He wondered what kind of bird it might be as he looked at Genevieve's long slim fingers. He wanted something, but he didn't know what. It was like an itch he couldn't reach to scratch. In the distance somewhere, he could hear people laughing and striking their croquet balls.

She reached out and touched his cheekbones lightly as if she were wiping away a speck of dirt. His throat hurt.

He wished the two of them could stay frozen in this moment. He let his fingertips move across her mouth for a long second. "Meet me tomorrow," he said.

"Where?"

"Here."

They began meeting everyday.

Of course, people found out. His intended fiancé stomped her foot and walked away when he entered a room. He didn't care as long as Genevieve was there.

His family was horrified. They forbid William to see her. He was destroying their plans for the future. Finding out what was happening, Genevieve's mother ordered her daughter to stay away from William. "You must not do this. We must find a suitable man from a good family for you."

"But William is suitable, Mama."

"But he is not available."

"But I love him!"

"I forbid you to see him ever again." Her face was so close to Genevieve's that she could count the hairs on her upper lip. "We will find someone else."

As many young couples before them, they ignored their elders and met in secret along the Hudson. Deciding they must be together, they planned to run away to New York City and be married. "After all, William," said Genevieve, dimpling up at him. "Once they see that we are married, they will have to agree that we are meant to be."

"Ah, Genevieve. I want this forever. I have always wanted you forever and ever."

She glanced at him. The coyness in her smile, the mischief in her eyes, and the tilt of her neck sent a wordless signal. Even nightfall, although it was only six hours away, felt like an eternity.

One May morning, as the lilacs were coming into bloom, they met by the river and hastened to Tarrytown, where they planned to catch the steamboat to New York. Unluckily, a servant from the young man's family saw them hurrying along the riverbank and reported them to his employers. William's father set out on his horse; his mother went to the Octagon House, where she accused Genevieve's mother of conspiring with the lovers. "My son will never marry your daughter. She is nothing but a pretty face. As for you, we will ostracize you."

The young couple made it on to the steamboat. Holding hands and making their plans, they sailed downstream. As the boat entered the shadow of the Palisades, its boiler burst, killing William instantly. Without her love, Genevieve knew that she no longer wanted to live. She sobbed to a fellow passenger, "William is no more. Mon Dieu! How can I live without him?"

The steamboat caught fire, and the boat began to sink midstream in the Hudson. That evening, when the bodies were all found, Genevieve's corpse was among them. Upset by the events of the last several days, Genevieve's mother refused to accept her dead body. Eventually, the beautiful daughter of great charm was buried in Potter's Field.

Supposedly, when the smell of lilacs is in the air, the ghost of a beautiful young woman wearing white has been seen walking around Octagon House.

Author's Note. Since 1978, Joseph Pell Lombardi, an architect specializing in historic preservation, has restored the house, a National Historic Landmark.

West Clinton Avenue
Irvington, New York

The Good Gray Ghost

All wars have some soldiers who return home to find their lives totally changed. New York State sent many young, native-born, men to war. In New York, they tell of the Good Gray Ghost, a soldier in the War Between the States, who was a familiar spirit in town.

When the War Between the States began in 1861, everyone was caught up in the war fever that swept the land that spring and summer. All over New York State, companies of militia were forming. Only three days after the surrender of Fort Sumter on April 18, large public rallies were held where more new men enlisted. By April 24, women in many towns and villages had vowed to sew the uniforms of the local company. As the cloth arrived, some women even sewed publicly in the town halls. Poets recited verses; flags waved; brass bands played. Those Yankee farmers, trades people, and artisans had become local heroes who would "whip the secesh" in a short time, or so they believed.

Men kissed wives, sons kissed mothers, and the girls wore their prettiest dresses, clinging to their handkerchiefs. Those who stayed at home urged their men to defend the Union to the death. And, of course, there was much talk of honor.

About fifty percent of all New Yorkers still lived on farms when the war began. Most farmers were not rich, but they were able to feed their own family and produce enough food to sell in the cities.

In the autumn, the fields are full of ripe pumpkins needing harvesting.
Courtesy of D. Peter Lund

One of the men who joined the Union force was a farmer named William Saunders. He kissed his wife, Helen, saying, "I have to go." He left home to be part of what he thought would be an exhilarating and ennobling experience. Hugging him hard, she said, "Mr. Sanders, my heart will beat anxiously for you and your well being, but I will tend to the home fires and care for our two children."

He patted her shoulder. He knew that she was proud of her man.

That first year was a hard year for Helen. She wasn't just knitting by the fireside and keeping the home fire burning; she and her children depended on her labor for their food, fuel, clothing, and home. She had to plow, cultivate, seed, weed, water, and harvest.

About a year later, Helen received a telegraph that William had been seriously wounded and was in a military hospital. That would be the last time she would hear of him.

Life was becoming harder for both Northerners and Southerners on the home front. The military needed everything that anyone could make so businesses that produced and sold food and other goods raised their prices. Helen, like many others, had to struggle to make ends meet. Each morning, she shouldered her hoe and walked to the field. At one point, life had held such promise, and now there was nothing. If she knew William were dead, she could accept it – or at least she thought she could. But he was missing, and that ambiguity overwhelmed her. It was hard to know when to give up hope and to begin grieving.

She felt weary, depressed, and totally worn down, trying to maintain the farm and provide food for her family. She wept endlessly. She wept when she fed the chickens, when she cooked for her children, and when she went to bed. She never heard herself crying. Her grief was a part of her, heard only in her bones like the sound of the winter wind moaning around the house. All she had was her children and a big demanding farm.

In need of help, she offered Isaac, a local man, room and board, if he would work the farm with her. As the months passed, she began to be aware again of the birds chirruping, the bees droning, and the butterflies darting among the flowers. In between all that harrowing, tilling, seeding, and harvesting, she saw a chance to shed her bitter unhappy self. She could begin life over again. Looking at Isaac, she felt something strong and solid that a woman could warm her hands and heart upon. So she married Isaac, who became a father to her children.

As the years passed, as each crop and beast followed its appointed time with the cows having their calves, the ewes dropping their kids, the corn being harvested, she felt thankful for her family and the presence of love in her life. A rounded and graceful fullness replaced her thinness. Smiles lit her face. A new baby filled the cradle.

In 1865, several months after the war had ended, a bearded, ragged man, wearing a tattered Union uniform, began to appear on the roads leading to town when the moon was bright. His hair hung long; his face was haggard.

Perhaps he had walked to his farm, contemplating the reunion that would have occurred if he hadn't died. His wife would have held him in her warm firm arms. He would stroke her long brown hair. They would slaughter a chicken and eat like he hadn't for years. When he arrived at the farm, however, he saw his wife bend her head toward the man besides her; he heard his children calling another man "Daddy." Yes, the Good Gray Ghost was home, but no one came to say "Hurrah, Hurrah" because he was long forgotten.

When Johnny comes marching home again,
Hurrah! Hurrah!
We'll give him a hearty welcome then
Hurrah! Hurrah!
The men will cheer and the boys will shout
The ladies they will all turn out
And we'll all feel gay,
When Johnny comes marching home.

– Patrick Sarsfield Gilmore

Capitol Ghosts

Albany, New York, is a powerful state capital with a strong presence in the national arena as well as in the state. Several U.S. Presidents have come from the New York statehouse; many New York state governors have contended for that role. Believed by many to be one of the most architecturally interesting government buildings in the country, New York State Capitol is a majestic granite building overlooking the Hudson River. Declared a National Historic Landmark in 1979, the building has its ghosts and its share of unexplainable events.

The creation of a number of architects, the New York State Capitol was under construction for more than twenty-five years. Several architects had worked on its design. British architect Thomas Fuller initiated the design in 1867. In 1874, local press attacked the design of the new Capitol Building, calling it the "White Elephant." Two prominent American architects, Leopold Eidlitz and Henry Hobson Richardson, replaced Fuller in the 1870s, which has led to a unique combination of Renaissance revival and Romanesque styles.

The capitol was built by hand. In places, its walls are four or five feet thick. When its construction began in 1874, electric lighting did not exist, and mechanical heating and ventilating were quite simplistic. Before it was completed, building technology had advanced significantly. The Capitol was lit by electricity, and heating technology had been incorporated into its design. Its cost, however, had exceeded 25 million dollars.

The building suffered a series of mishaps. Before it was complete, an Irish plasterer decided to work late one night on the new Assembly Chamber ceiling. High on a scaffold underneath the arched ceiling, he labored alone. At some point, he plunged to the stone floor forty feet below. He died three days later.

Governor Theodore Roosevelt declared the New York State Capitol complete in 1899. In 1911, the night watchman, Sam Abbott, walked the third and fourth floor of the building – not far from where the plasterer had fallen. He smelled some smoke but saw nothing until he opened a door. According to the *New York Times* (March 30, 1911), 100,000 books, 400,000 pamphlets, 300,000 manuscripts, and the sacred wampum of the Six Nations in the State Library were lost in the fire – one of the greatest library disasters of modern times. Sam Abbott may have died of smoke inhalation, but he has not given up guarding the building. People say that his spirit keeps watch in the library and the nearby hall. Staff members talk about feeling chills or something brushing up against them when they are working. Some say Sam Abbott dressed in the same way he was the night he died still makes his nightly rounds.

In 1887, an assemblyman just missed being hit by a seven-pound chunk of stone dropping from the arched assembly chamber ceiling. Years later, water seeped through the ceiling and discolored two murals on the upper walls. A new, flat wooden ceiling was built twenty feet below the previous one, forever sealing the original murals from public view.

The cornerstone of the building, which contains copies of all the legislation relating to the Capitol, various U.S. coins and currency of 1871, and Albany newspapers of that year, cannot be found today. The builders forgot to mark it.

In recent years, cleaners have felt that unseen others are watching them at their work. In 1990, one night cleaner came back to his mop and bucket to find his mop cleaning the floor. Strangers in old-fashioned clothing have been seen, and, of course, there are the usual cold drafts. Many who work on the fifth floor overnight quickly request transfers somewhere else, or refuse to work there.

Perhaps the hard-working plasterer and Sam Abbott are still working the late shift!

Washington Avenue and State Street Albany, New York

The Party at Shelter Island

Shelter Island is nestled between rural North Fork and posh South Fork of Long Island. Surrounded by the Peconic, Gardener's and Shelter Island Bays, this 8,000-acre area offers pristine beaches, breathtaking water views, historic homes, hideaway inns, gourmet eateries, and a haunted house.

Shelter Island isn't all that big, but it has substantial history. In 1652, Nathaniel Sylvester, a wealthy sugar merchant from Barbados, settled here with his sixteen-year-old bride, Grissel. Supporters of Charles I, they were royalist refugees from Oliver Cromwell's England. Consequently, the Sylvesters' social life was centered in Newport, where other political refugees loyal to the Stuart monarchy had found safety. When the monarchy was restored in England, they were granted the land, and by 1673, Nathaniel owned the entire island. Following his death, the island was divided among his heirs and further divided and sold until it was incorporated in 1730. At the time of the American Revolution, Sag Harbor was a strategic port to the British who captured Long Island early in the war. The British shipped hay from Hay Beach, and British occupiers decimated much of Shelter Island's landscape. During the War of 1812, the British ransacked numerous homes on the island.

Throughout the nineteenth century, many residents worked in the whaling, shipbuilding, and fishing industries and a number of men enlisted in the Northern army during the Civil War. In 1871, the Shelter Island Grove and Camp Meeting Association of the Methodist Episcopal Church began to develop the island as a summer resort. As the population grew, a road was completed connecting two commercial ferries. Today, there are approximately 2,500 full time residents, and the population triples during the summer.

But the original families are still represented here. Many families can claim vacationing here continuously for five generations, and the widow of a descendant of Nathaniel Sylvester resides in the Manor House, built in 1733 by Nathaniel Sylvester's grandson.

Now to return to our ghost. On Shelter Island, there is a house owned by a family, which has owned the land since the reign of Charles II of England. The family members, dead or alive, have a habit of returning to the house, which certainly can startle people not in the know.

Late in the evening on holidays and family birthdays, according to the locals, the two senior owners stand by the head of their stairs and listen to their long dead relatives enjoying their parties on the main floor. The champagne corks pop, the silver scrapes on the good china, the violins and harps play, and the laughter pours up the stairwells. No one in the house fears death, for to die means only that they would join the family at their party in the dining room.

Once a niece came to visit with a young doctor, whom she thought she might marry. He was a very scientific young man who didn't believe in any superstitious nonsense. One morning, he was shaving, when he suddenly saw another face beside his own – an old lady. He turned about quickly, but there was no old lady watching him. He returned to his task. Several minutes later, after some more careful strokes of the razor, the face appeared again. When he completed his task, he complained about the incident to his hostess.

She responded happy, "Oh yes, the family relatives do come around. We don't have male visitors here very often any more."

The Pink House

In the town of Wellsville stands a lovely Italianate Victorian pink house. A local landmark, it figures in several ghost stories revolving about an early suicide in the house. In 1898, Hanford Lennox Gordon wrote a poem, "Pauline," about the circumstances leading up to the suicide.

Once upon a time, a cruel lumber merchant, who was notorious for his heartless and cold manner, owned the lovely pink house. People cringed when they saw him. The only thing he loved was his daughter, Pauline. All was well as long as he was first in Pauline's affections. Then, one day, Pauline fell in love with Paul, the son of a poor widow, who lived on the outskirts of town in a pitiful shack. When Paul's mother died, Pauline comforted him, pledging her love for him.

Paul resolved that with Pauline's love he could escape from his humble beginnings. He would go to a distant relative in the East to study and become a lawyer. The young couple managed to keep their romance a secret from her disapproving father for several years. Then the very day that Paul was to leave the village to study law, her father caught them embracing. Pauline's father castigated Paul, "How dare you even look at my daughter? She is not for you."

Pauline begged him to stop. "Father," she pled. "Father, please. I love him."

But her father wiped his mouth with his handkerchief and walked away. Paul went to law school, and for four long years the couple continued to communicate by letter. Finally, Pauline's father forged a "Dear John" letter from Pauline to Paul and a betrayal letter from Paul to her. Those letters had the desired result, effectively stopping their correspondence and leaving both of them hurt and angry.

A year later, Pauline became engaged to rich, middle-aged Mr. Hall, whom she did not love, but whom her father encouraged her to wed for financial reasons. On the day before she was to be married, she passed Paul on the main street of Wellsville. Paul, who was still anguished by her "Dear John" letter, ignored her completely. That night, he dreamed that he saw her "in the silent night leaning o'er misty waters dark and deep; A moan – a splash of waters – and O Christ – Her agonized face upturned – imploring hands stretched out toward me, and a wailing cry – Paul, O Paul." (Gordon, p. 106)

In the morning, he learned that Pauline committed suicide in the now-filled fountain in front of the Pink House. Later that day, he received a letter from her, which enclosed the forged betrayal letter.

From then on, Pink House began to show signs of being haunted. People would enter a room and have a feeling that a woman had just left it by another door. At night, the piano would play Pauline's favorite pieces. Her perfume would hover within the room.

In some variations of this story, Paul marries her sister, and Pauline drowns herself in a millpond. Sometimes, her ghost lures her little niece into the fountain, where the child loses her life.

Author's Note: According to historians, the young woman who committed suicide in 1857 was Frances Farnum. Hanford Lennox Gordon called her Pauline in his poem by the same name.

The Ghost of Love

The Thousand Islands Region, encompassing communities on both sides of the American and Canadian border along the St. Lawrence River and the eastern shores of Lake Ontario, is known for its spectacular natural beauty. The Native Americans called the region "Manatoana" or Garden of the Great Spirit. Today, it is named for the many more than thousand islands that line this international waterway.

Both the Iroquois and Algonquin traveled to this area for hunting and fishing. After the Native Americans came the squatters, smugglers, lumbermen and then the shipbuilders. The French explorers named the region. Soon after the Civil War as transportation developed, sportsmen began to travel to Alexandria Bay, New York, located in the heart of the area for the fishing. Ultimately, wealthy vacationers from New York City, Chicago, and other American and Canadian cities discovered the region in that opulent, pre income tax period, 1874 – 1912.

Known for inventing railroad sleeping cars, George M. Pullman invited General Grant to his Thousand Islands home in 1872. The media traveled with Grant, who was running for President of the United States. Once the press began writing articles about this hunting and fishing paradise, people wanted to visit. As many as twenty trains a day would come and go at the village stations. Passengers and their many trunks (no carry-ons in those days!) would transfer from train to steamship to their island destinations. The city servants would bring a family's trunks and luggage, and local summer help would be hired. Recreational excursion vessels and local steamboat lines were introduced to the area. The large vessels served not merely transient tourists but also gave access to many new island and mainland resort communities.

The small communities along the United States and Canadian shores supplied labor to build new hotels and grandiose "summer "cottages. Horse drawn carts transported building materials over the ice in the winter. Hotels were built, and bankers, heads of industry, lawyers, robber barons, and social leaders built many fabulous summer homes on the Thousand Islands. Several still exist. One of the most famous is Boldt Castle, which is ranked by *Almanac of Architecture and Design* as the fourteenth most popular historic house museum.

When he was thirteen years old, George C. Boldt emigrated from Prussia to the United States all by himself. Beginning work as a dishwasher in the kitchen of the Merchants' Exchange Hotel, he so impressed his bosses that he quickly advanced, working his way up the hotel management ladder. When he met the lovely fragile Louise Augusta Kehrer, of Philadelphia, Pennsylvania, he was twenty-six and she was fifteen. They were married in 1877.

George was a hard-working man of tremendous talent. He developed several Philadelphia hotels, eventually owning the Bellevue-Stratford, and became the manager of William Astor's Waldorf hotel in New York in 1893. He was the president of several other companies, a trustee of Cornell University, and the director of the Hotel Association of New York.

A hotel magnate, he built his fortune on new standards of hospitality. Supposedly, he came to the attention of William Waldorf Astoria, when an Astor relative took a sick child to a New Jersey resort where he had a small hotel. There were no rooms available, so George and Louise gave up their room to the child, who recovered. In his gratitude, the relative persuaded William Waldorf Astoria to build the Waldorf, which became the epitome of a good hotel. When the magnificent new hotel opened in 1893, it only had thirty-two guests. Three months later, it was immensely successful.

George's philosophy of hotel management centered on his guests; he believed that a patron should never leave the premises unsatisfied. His wife, Louise, was deeply involved in the hotel business, purchasing furnishings from Europe for the Waldorf and overseeing their placement. She provided what was called a "woman's touch," ensuring that all of the bedrooms had fresh flowers and a candle in case the lights failed. Together, they made the Waldorf Hotel an overwhelming success.

Within five years, the hotel was so popular that John Jacob Astor, William Waldorf Astor's cousin, built the second half of the hotel, which became know as the Waldorf-Astoria.

Building of the Castle

George adored his wife, whom he treated like a princess. In 1893, George and Louise and their two children vacationed in Alexandria Bay and immediately fell in love with the area. He liked the area so much that he often entertained his friends and business associates there; they, in turn, built their summerhouses on the islands. He also bought land in the region, including several hundred acres on Wellesley Island.

Supposedly, on one vacation, Oscar Tschirky, George Boldt's steward on his yacht "Louise" (named after Mrs. Boldt) discovered that the salad for the noon meal had been left behind. Improvising with the ingredients he had on board the yacht, the steward quickly created the now world-renowned Thousand Island dressing. George Boldt so enjoyed it that he began to serve it at his hotels. The creative steward was promoted to work at the Waldorf Astoria and subsequently rose to international fame as "Oscar of the Waldorf."

In 1895, Louisa Boldt bought Heart Island (then called Hart Island) for one dollar. The family spent several summers on Heart Island in the old summer cottage, while they made improvements. They built the powerhouse to provide electricity to island buildings and the Hennery, or dovecote, to house George's favorite birds. In 1899, they built Alster Tower or the "Playhouse," which contained a billiard room, library, kitchen, ballroom, and several apartments. In the basement was a two-lane bowling alley!

The 90-foot Alster Tower or "Playhouse" overlooks the St. Lawrence River. The whimsical building was intended for the entertainment of guests and the Boldt children. *Courtesy of D. Peter Lund*

Opposite Page:
The castle is adorned with symbols of hearts as testimony to George Boldt's love for his wife. *Courtesy of D. Peter Lund*

The six-story, 120-room Boldt Castle is modeled after sixteenth century buildings. It combines the beauty of medieval towers with large, plate glass windows, wrap-around porches, an elevator, and fireproof construction. *Courtesy of D. Peter Lund*

But a mere Playhouse wasn't sufficient to express George's love. In September 1899, George Boldt announced that he planned to build a castle on Heart Island as a gift of love for his adored Louise. The old summer cottage, "Hart House," was slid in sections across the frozen St. Lawrence River, to become the Wellesley House and part of the Thousand Islands Country Club. George altered the shape of the island into a heart-shape, added a lagoon, and changed the spelling to Heart Island, which remains today. Throughout the castle, hearts abound. He planned to present the finished product to Louise on Valentine's Day, her birthday.

The quiet Heart Island became a hubbub of activity. Over 300 of the best artists and master craftsmen, landscape gardeners, electricians, and masons, using the very best materials, were hired to build his castle, which would be modeled after those in Rhineland, Germany. Hewitt and Hewitt of Philadelphia designed the 170- x 160-foot six-story castle with its 2 foot thick walls. It contained 127 rooms with 30 bathrooms, 16 fireplaces, and 365 windows covered by 30,000 square feet of roof tile.

Unlike many construction projects, money was not a problem. The army of workmen didn't overlook a single detail called for in this monumental work of architecture that was to be George's gift to Louise. Approximately 150 laborers quarried stone from George Boldt's own Oak Island to supply the requisite stone. The completed castle would include an indoor pool, sixteen fireplaces, a powerhouse, a drawbridge, Italian gardens, a swan pond, a three-story dovecote, a Roman archway that was to be the formal entry for launches delivering guests to the island, and service tunnels equipped with trolleys.

The Boldts spent their summers in Alster Tower while work was progressing on the castle. In January of 1904, after four years of construction, the castle was nearing completion. Pink and white Italian marble, European sculptures, carving, mosaics, and tapestries were purchased.

But one day in 1904, George wired the workers to immediately "stop all construction" as Louise, at age forty-one, had died suddenly. The island fell into an eerie silence, as 300 workers put down their hammers and went home, leaving behind the unfinished structure for almost three-quarters of a century. George never returned to the island, leaving behind the unfinished structure as a monument of his love. When George died at age sixty-five in 1916, people said that, more than any other man, he was responsible for the modern American hotel. Despite his reputation as a hotel magnate, his heart remained broken.

Once the scene of a major love, the castle became deserted and quietly slid into decay. For generations, the castle stood empty. Its massive fireplaces and ornate plaster ceilings cracked and fell away. Beams collapsed, windows disappeared. Its rooms opened to wildlife, birds, and the skies. Only the ghost of a great love and the occasional vandals inhabited it. In 1939, the roof of the Power House, Clock and Chimes Tower burned down. Eventually, the solid stonewalls of the roofless building slowly gave way and fell into the waters of the St. Lawrence River below. In 1942, as part of the war effort, workers removed tons of scrap iron and steel from the island, stripping the castle of the decorative ironwork, the elaborate heating systems, and thousands of feet of piping. The once beautiful, almost complete castle stood imprisoned by the past, caked with layers of psychic dust.

Of course, there was talk of ghosts, but the major ghost was that of the love George had for Louise.

In 1977, the Thousand Islands Bridge Authority acquired the property and decided to rehabilitate, restore, and improve Boldt Castle and its structures. Since then, George's architectural dream has attracted over 5 million visitors and 700 weddings to the region.

Thousand Island Dressing

Mix together 1 1/4 cups mayonnaise, 1/3 cup ketchup, 1 tbsp lemon juice, 2 tbsp capers, 3 tbsp chopped scallions, 3 tbsp chopped dill pickle, 1 large hard-boiled egg, finely chopped (optional), 1 tbsp Dijon mustard, dash Tabasco, season with salt and pepper.

Heart Island, Alexandria Bay, New York

The Haunting of Big Moose Lake

The proximity of the Adirondacks to New York and Boston made them an appealing destination in the nineteenth century. Once the railway was built, many New Yorkers and Bostonians began vacationing in the Adirondacks. Entrepreneurs built a number of Adirondack hotels, while those with money constructed large estates complete with hunting lodges, icehouses, carriage houses, and boathouses. They're known as "camps." Most people thought the Adirondacks region where the air and water were pristine was beneficial. Some, such as young Grace Brown, found that a trip to the breathtaking scenery of the Adirondacks was not so beneficial.

My home has always been Big Moose Lake. I love its big pines, the lake, and the beauty of all those woods. I like the sound of the ice cracking, the smell of new fallen snow, and the excitement of the first green shoots in the spring. There aren't many roads to the lake so we really only see people during June-August when the lake and the sky turn so blue that it almost stops your breath. That's the time when New Yorkers and Bostonians come to hunt, boat, play croquet, drink fine wines, talk about their fishing exploits, and enjoy the setting. Although the summer people often bring their servants, they also employ the local people during their stay. We work as guides, maids, drivers, caretakers, and handymen, foregoing our usual hardscrabble existence for the brief time that the tourists are here.

But in September, when they leave, we are just a small town of woodsmen and homesteaders hoping to get through the long gray winter. The lake completely freezes over, the deer strip all the lower branches hanging over the lake, the sky turns dull gray, and the cold sets in. Then the first sleet sifts through the forest branches, the wind rattles the frozen branches, and the snow appears like a ghost in the silent night, shrouding the fields and hills in a soft white.

During the winter, I make some money by checking on the homes of the rich people, the "camps" they call them, and making sure everything is all right – that there aren't any leaks or animals in the buildings. During the season, I do some guiding and rent rowboats on the lake for the big hotels. And that is how I got my few brief moments of fame.

That hot July day, I saw this young couple approaching me. She was clinging tightly to his arm, like she couldn't let him go. He was pretty slick in his straw hat, asking me if he could rent a boat. I asked, "Are you experienced at handling one?"

"Of course," he said. Tiny globes of sweat, no bigger than pinheads, dotted his upper lip. I fetched him a rowboat.

The Adirondacks contain over 100 summits, ranging from under 1,200 to over 5,000 feet in altitude and 2,000 miles of hiking trails. They have over 2,300 lakes and ponds and 1,500 miles of rivers. Thirty thousand miles of brooks and streams run within the area. *Courtesy of D. Peter Lund*

Courtesy of D. Peter Lund

She stepped in very carefully, holding hard to his hand, saying, "Hold me tight now, Chester. You know I can't swim." A blue vein pulsed in her neck.

He snapped at her, "I know that, Grace, you've told me that at least one hundred times." She looked like she was going to cry. After helping her in, he did a strange thing . He put a suitcase and a tennis racket into the stern. If he was planning to spend a night on a deserted beach with her, he didn't need a suitcase but a blanket! It can get cold around here. And what was with the tennis racket? There weren't any tennis courts down near the lake.

Later, people said they had seen them on the lake that day, but they didn't come back that night so I figured that they found some place to stay and that was why they needed the suitcase. Sometimes tourists don't realize how big the lake is and how quickly night comes. All those pines make it really dark up here, and she was a pretty little thing.

When they didn't return the next day, I got worried. I stewed around for a bit, then gathered up some other guides, and we got on the steamboat and started to search the lake. Finally, we spotted an overturned rowboat.

When we got over to it and I identified it as mine, young Joey who had come along spotted something odd on the lake's bottom. He kept pointing, "Look, look." We ignored the kid, but he became so persistent that one of the guys lowered a long spiked pole and poked around in the weeds at some murky object before hauling this thing up through the waters.

First thing I saw was a pale white arm drifting around like a strange underwater weed. Then I saw the head, which looked all bruised, and there was an ugly cut on her face. It was the young woman from the day before, Grace. We hauled her up and raced towards shore. One of the men with me carried her up the path in his arms. The water dripped from her, and her dress clung to her body.

The young man was missing. We went back to see if we could find his body but had no luck. We hoped out loud that he was still alive.

Someone called the sheriff. The newspapermen began crowding into town. Violent death sells newspapers after all, one told me. It came out quickly that the couple was staying at the Glenmore Hotel. I should have known that this slick young man would have picked the Glenmore. It has been popular since the early 1800s with high-class types, corporate big wigs, and many celebrities. While on his hunting vacations, Vice President Theodore Roosevelt frequently lodged at the Glenmore Hotel. He was coming here on the train when he was told of President McKinley's death and sworn in as twenty-sixth president. But let me get back to my story. After we found the body, the hotel and the cottages were full of reporters from the city papers.

When the police checked the hotel registration, they learned that the young man was "Carl Grahm of Albany," and she was "Grace Brown of South Otselic." One of the newspapermen discovered that Grace Brown was an employee of the Gillette Skirt Factory in Cortland, New York. She came from a farm family from Chenango County in New York, he said. A cute little thing, she had told everyone at the factory that she wanted to get away from life on the farm and have some fun. Originally, she moved to Cortland to babysit for her older sister, but she wanted more excitement then someone else's baby, so she went to work in the factory. There she met the owner's good-looking nephew, Chester Gillette, and one thing led to another. So guess who Carl Grahm was? Chester Gillette himself. By spring, he had put poor Grace in the family way. There was no way that the ambitious nephew of the owner was going to be serious about a farm girl, but try to convince a young pregnant girl of that!

She returned to her parents' home in South Otselic, where she bombarded Chester with letters about making her an honest woman. Of course, our good-looking Chester stayed in Cortland, where he happily saw other women. It didn't look like Chester was going to make an honest woman out of her, but she was persistent. Of course, she was fighting for herself and her baby. She kept writing him, hinting that his life would be ruined, too.

Finally, Chester gave in to her demands and told her he had made arrangements for a trip for the two of them to the Adirondacks. After spending July 9, 1906, in Utica, they took the train to Tupper Lake, where they spent their second night together. On the morning of July 11, they took the train back towards Utica and stopped at Glenmore Hotel at Big Moose Lake, which is where I met them.

When he registered at Glenmore Hotel, good old Chester used a false name (one that matched his initials on his suitcase monogram) when they registered. He brought little luggage with him. Guess he knew he wasn't going to be staying long. Grace, who probably expected that he had seen the light and would make her an honest woman, brought her entire wardrobe. But she never got to wear any of those clothes because he took her on that fatal boat ride.

They found him three days later with his suitcase at Arrowhead Hotel, where the police arrested him. By Saturday, July 14, all the local newspapers reported news of Grace's death. Grace's trunk contained a pile of letters from Chester. When asked, Chester admitted they were from him and told them that he had all of Grace's letters *to him* in his lodgings in Cortland.

In one of those letters, she told Chester that she couldn't swim. That shows you how naïve Grace was. You never tell a guy you can't swim, especially if you're in the family way and he's ignoring you. So they said that Gillette had beaten her over the head with tennis racket until she fell in. That was why she was all bruised.

Chester said he had taken Grace out on Big Moose Lake but insisted that she had accidentally drowned. He was found guilty and died in the electric chair in Auburn Prison on March 30, 1908, at 6:15 a.m.

People say they have witnessed a white female floating just above the surface of the lake. Others report experiencing great feelings of sadness while visiting the lake. Researchers believe that Grace's death, coupled with the death of her unborn child, came at such an early age that she has not been able to pass over. I don't know what I believe, but I do know that since her death, the light in the woods seems to be thicker, stripping away the world I know. The dank lake air muffles the birdcalls, and the afternoon mist sets in earlier. And out of the corner of my eye, I've noticed frightening flickering shadows slipping in and out of the woods. I don't feel so safe in the woods anymore.

And that's the end of my sad tale of Grace Brown who wanted some excitement and got far more than she bargained for.

Away from the sight of people
Where nobody heard her last call,
Or no one could tell how it happened
But God - and Gillette - knows all.

Author's Note. Of course, no one knows what exactly happened that dark night on Big Moose Lake, but various people have their own ideas. Some such as Theodore Dreiser wrote a book about the events; his *An American Tragedy* was later adapted as a movie, *A Place In The Sun*, which won six Oscars. Meanwhile, many visit Big Moose Lake, hoping to see the ghost of Grace.

Big Moose Lake
New York

Silver Screens of the Past

Small movie theaters are a relic of the past. Now, we have 6-screen stadium-style seating multiplex cinemas. But some of those single screen theaters were grand palaces.

Silent movies arrived in Syracuse in the early twentieth century. There was the Empire, the Strand, Keith's, Temple (later Paramount), and Eckel theatres, but the grandest, with 3,000 seats, was Loew's State Theatre designed by Thomas W. Lamb. Today, it is the city's only surviving example of the opulent theatrical venues of the 1920s. Now named "The Landmark," the theater is on the National Register of Historic Places.

Opened on February 18, 1928, it was advertised as "the last word in theatrical ornateness and luxuriousness." By mid-morning on that first day, hundreds had formed lines outside, where they were greeted by a uniformed doorman or "barker." Overseen by uniformed captains, uniformed ushers directed eager customers into lines between velvet ropes through the marble lobbies with their ornate tapestries, elaborate chandeliers, and exotic furnishings. The main lobby sported a Tiffany chandelier and the grandest of the theatre's several huge murals. Patrons who ascended the grand staircase reached the promenade lobby, where they found a fishpond with a Japanese pagoda fountain. Decorated in rich reds and gold, the main auditorium was accented with wall ornaments throughout. The 1,400-pipe Wurlitzer organ provided such exotic sounds as a glockenspiel, marimba, bird whistles, hoof beats, and surf sounds. The Musician's Gallery, located over the front doors, featured quartet serenades as intermission entertainment during the 1930s. Sharply dressed "candy girls" graced the concession counters.

Loew's showed its first "talkie, *The Broadway Melody*, on March 30, 1929. During the Depression and World War II, theater patrons would flee reality and enjoy the grandeur of Hollywood. In 1934, the theater introduced double features, and color films became available. In the early 1940s, it showed war films and newsreels. Veterans paraded across the stage. Intermissions were devoted to war bond sales.

After World War II, the theater began to suffer from increasing staffing and maintenance costs and taxes. Mechanical plants failed. Decorative fabrics, walls, carpeting, and seating, once fastidiously maintained, fell victim to vandalism. The wonderful organ was sold as was the main lobby chandelier. By 1976, the owners were considering razing the theater.

On July 9, the Syracuse Area Landmark Theatre (SALT) was designated the agency to try to acquire and preserve the theatre. The city promised tax rebates. With the help of a benefit concert by Harry Chapin, the group successfully raised the money to purchase the property and begin the work of restoration, at which time Loew's State was renamed the Landmark Theatre.

As the group began to restore the theater, they discovered that the rumors of a resident ghost in the theater were based on fact. A pallid young woman dressed in white was often seen threading her way through the middle balcony. Sometimes she was seen near the restrooms, leading to people wondering whether ghosts had the same bodily needs as humans. Stagehands also heard a woman's voice calling them by their names.

Several staff members brought in a local psychic, who said the ghost's name was Claire. Claire had been married to a Loew's employee and always wanted to be an actress, but never got very far. Apparently, she died before she actually was in a performance, so she took up directing in her afterlife – supervising all performances from the balcony!

Still open today, the Landmark offers concerts and other performances, is available for weddings and other private parties, and continues to sponsor fundraisers to support its activities. According to Peter Baum of SALT, Loew's State was the first great "Oriental-style" movie theater, predating Grauman's Chinese Theater in Hollywood, California, and two additional Loew's "Oriental palaces" in New York City.

362 South Salina Street
Syracuse, New York

Woman in White

Many old mansions, which often have been transformed into modern inns, have ghosts. Perhaps the specters like the smell of good food, the tinkle of silverware, and the talk of patrons. This haunted inn has a ghost who doesn't like people to drink.

Built in 1802, the Bull's Head Inn is housed in a beautiful setting with magnificent manicured grounds. Before 1838, the inn was used as a town hall, a courthouse, and a public meeting place. The local Dutch and German farmers didn't spend much time or money in taverns so an owner converted the building back into a home again. In 1960, it was opened again as an inn.

Constructed in the Federal Georgian style, it is the oldest building in the quaint Dutch Colonial village of Cobleskill. A formal garden with a stylish fountain at the center lies behind the restaurant. It has archways, a tiny waterfall, and small benches. Flowers, herbs, and shrubbery are well tended and neatly trimmed.

The interior is just as inviting. A lively bar occupies the front room with the main dining room off to the right. Classical paintings, each individually lit, feature horse scenes from the area; a few depict old-fashioned fox hunts. Tablecloths are starched, napkins are neatly folded, candles are lit and a peppermill on each table shows that this restaurant is serious about its atmosphere.

The inn certainly has atmosphere. Some staffers say that at the end of the evening when the last customers have left, they often go to the tavern downstairs for a final drink. That is when they hear someone walking upstairs. The usual ghost happenings occur here, frightening some, and amusing others. Silverware, china, and napkins fly through the air; strange noises occur spontaneously; empty captain's chairs swivel on their own.

Their most famous ghost is a former member of the Women's Christian Temperance Union (WCTU). After 1920, John Stacy, who thoroughly enjoyed his drink, owned the inn. Concerned about the destructive power of alcohol, Mrs. Stacy tried to combat its influence on her husband. Before her death, she became a staunch member of the WCTU. When her bedroom became a dining room and bar in 1962, her ghost was outraged. She began to appear in a long, white filmy gown. According to the waitresses and bartenders, she would walk through the tables, chairs, and walls of the room. Occasionally, her specter was so angry that it picked up pieces of silverware from the tables and threw them at the bar. Mrs. Stacy has not created enough mischief yet to close down the bar. Actually, her presence seems to add interest and appeal to Bull's Head Inn.

2 Park Place Cobleskill New York

The Great White Way

In the 1890s, new and sumptuous theaters decorated with glittering crystal chandeliers and gilded interiors were being built throughout New York's theatrical district. Patrons thronged to the theaters to enjoy drawing room drama, naughty French farce, and musical revues. Theater owner-producers like David Belasco, Oscar Hammerstein, Florenz Ziegfeld, and the Schuberts attracted affluent middle-class patrons to their new theaters. Splashed in a sea of electric lights, these theaters and other palaces transformed Broadway into the Great White Way. Once the theaters closed their curtains, Broadway became a chaos of private carriages, ad buses, hired coaches, and cabs. After a night at the theater, the wealthy stockbrokers and businessmen, the "men about town," the theatrical celebrities, the chorus girls, and those seeking escape from the oppressive stuffiness of high society would return to the Broadway restaurants.

I always loved the theater. My grandmother even knew someone from the old days who took me up one of the ladders into the flies – that's what they call them – so I could perch on the crosswalks and have a perfect view of the stage. When I made it to the top, I stood on a small platform holding onto a ladder that disappeared into the darkness as it continued further up. A narrow walkway spanning the stage was at eye level with me; behind it, various backdrops hung, waiting for their turn to be dropped. I was high enough that I didn't feel safe letting go of the ladder.

Later, I came down to ground, and my grandmother took me to the Russian Tea Room, and I asked her about working in the theater, "Ah yes," said grandmother, dramatically punctuating her sentences with her long pointed fingernails. "Times Square was the Bright Light Zone, the Crossroads of the World, the Great White Way. When I was a girl, it was the site of everything magical. And, of course, there are ghosts there, too."

"Really, ghosts? On Broadway?"

"Certainly."

"So tell me about one of the ghosts." My grandmother loved to talk.

One of the most famous, she said, was the Bishop of Broadway, David Belasco. Known for his scenic realism, he helped modernize the American stage. He opened the Stuyvesant Theater at 111-21 West 44th Street on October 16, 1907 with 1,030 seats. The Belasco was a magnificent building – more a palace than just a theater. In 1910, when he had sold his other theater, he renamed this theater for himself.

"So he was famous?"

"My dear, he was what was known as an impresario – one of the major pioneers in the theater. He had this brilliant idea that the auditorium of the Belasco Theatre was like a living room, even though it seated more than one thousand people. Can you imagine?"

I couldn't.

She resumed, "He knew that theater was much better when the actors were closer to the audience. The audience likes to be close to the actors – to see the sweat dripping from their faces, their spittle spewing." Does spittle really spew? I wondered. She went on, "He could create that theatrical intimacy by bringing the stage closer, which meant making the auditorium less deep."

Seating 1,018, the Belasco Theater is one of the Great White Way Broadway theaters. *Courtesy of D. Peter Lund*

"Anything else?"

"He also knew how to create and manage stage effects. He knew what looked real. The rich walnut paneling, ornamental Tiffany lamps, and eighteen mural panels created a grand setting for Belasco's mix of dazzling scenic effects and melodrama. Each of the ceiling panels held a domed lighting unit bearing the painted coat of arms of a person or place significant in theatrical history. Known for his sumptuous realistic productions, Belasco was involved with every facet of that theater. He set the standard – from Louis Hartman's state-of-the-art lighting board capable of producing magical effects, to replacing onstage footlights with spotlights from the auditorium, to the freight elevator that we used to bring up the scenery and props from the basement shops. Modern theatrical design began with him, so to speak. Quite the "man of the new century."

"When he was working with Henry de Mille, he would pace the stage, acting out the beginnings of the play. Henry would take notes and then go write something. Belasco would polish it in rehearsal. He had the touch, you know. For example, he wrote the play of *Madame Butterfly* to fill out an evening featuring the farce *Naughty Anthony*, which premiered in March 1900 at the Herald Square Theater. It was such a great success that seven weeks later, Belasco took a three-act version to London. That was so successful that Miacomo Puccini noticed it. And he later composed the immortal opera "Madama Butterfly."

"Belasco was the one who added the part where Butterfly stands alone on stage, waiting for Pinkerton as stage lights showed the passing of the night. Although the play was based on a short story written by another person, Belasco was the one who decided that Butterfly should kill herself and that Pinkerton would arrive just in time to cradle her in his arms as she died."

"He knew how to make something romantic."

"Yes, David was known as the silver-haired wizard of Broadway. He produced and directed nearly fifty shows, many of which he also wrote. He was always working, perhaps that is why he is said to haunt the theater still."

"Where does this haunt hang out?"

"Well, that's the more salacious part of my tale. As you may recall, Belasco was called The Bishop of Broadway because he liked to wear a clerical collar and cassock, and he spent almost all of his time working at the Belasco when he wasn't wooing his actresses. Today, we might call him a workaholic.

"Of course, a theater can be dreadfully spooky: scenery flats, costumes, ropes, spotlights, and always the props waiting to be used. A stage light left on when the theater is completely deserted is called a ghost light. Legend says that it is there for the ghosts to perform their plays or maybe for stage directors to lure young women to their private rooms.

"Some say Belasco was quite the rake. Many beautiful actresses found their way to his ten-room apartment above the theatre. Technically, he was married, but his apartment was the city's supreme bachelor pad, configured and employed for the seduction of leading and not-so-leading ladies. An elevator took the girls straight up from backstage to a watery vestibule called the Grotto [this was before Hugh Hefner was even born, mind you!]. They passed into an ornate study, where the Bishop of Broadway, as he was known, awaited them, in clerical dress. The pornography was hidden behind sliding panels in the wainscoting of the bedroom upstairs. Decorated like a Gothic church, the apartment housed a bizarre collection of theatrical loot – a pew from Shakespeare's church, a lock of Napoleon's hair, and a theatrical library. Today, that collection is long gone, but, according to a recent *New Yorker* article (February 9, 2009) the old paneled cupboards still stand in the gloom and soot."

"So," I yawned, "what about the ghost?"

"That's the best part. Wearing a clerical collar, Belasco allegedly began to appear consistently after his death in 1931. People knew it was Belasco because they could smell his cigar smoke. Others claim that they saw him wearing his collar sitting in the back of the theater at openings of new shows. Of course, many have reported hearing footsteps, despite the motion sensors and high security. Closed doors open and no one is there. Even the disconnected elevator runs, although no one pushes its buttons."

"That's great. Is the ghost still appearing?"

"The last big sighting of Belasco's ghost occurred at a performance of *Oh! Calcutta!* in 1972; in the middle of the show, it left its customary seat, in the balcony. The presumption was that it had been offended by the play's salaciousness, but this hardly seems likely, since Belasco, in life, was, among many other things, a legendary lady's man."

"Is he the only ghost in that theater?"

"The other ghost is that of a showgirl in a blue dress, who is thought by some to have been Belasco's girlfriend. Known as the Blue Lady, she supposedly died when she fell into an elevator shaft backstage. She appears as a blue light floating up from the balcony, as a blur of blue ascending the steps to Belasco's apartment, or as a woman wearing a blue gown."

Supposedly, the ghost of the Blue Lady is not seen when the dramatic productions feature a woman in a blue dress. In *Awake and Sing!* the Clifford Odets revival that finished its run at the Belasco in February 2009, that role belonged to Zoë Wanamaker. Because of this policy of appeasing the ghost, modern day viewers rarely see the Blue Lady!

111 West 44 Street
New York, New York

The Lost City

Kings Park State Hospital has been associated with many legends and ghost stories. It is easy to imagine ghosts here when you think of all the mentally ill patients and the hundreds of staff members who have called this place home over the years. It is even easier when you look at empty buildings with windows full of hidden eyes. The murmuring of the wind in the trees, the sighing sound it makes blowing through the area warns one to leave.

In 1885, Brooklyn established a facility for mentally ill patients on land purchased from a group of Smithtown land owners along the Nissequoque River. Originally, three wooden buildings housed 55 patients on 800 acres of former farmland. The hospital was a "Farm Colony" asylum, which was at the cutting edge of treatment for the mentally ill in those days. Farm-related activities, such as feeding livestock and growing food, were considered to be a form of therapy at the time. As part of the "work is therapy" philosophy, the asylum provided opportunities for patients to gain a sense of purpose through farming, construction, and other trades that kept the institution fully self-sufficient.

Within ten years, the "Lunatic Farm" became overcrowded. The facility was transferred to the state, and, for the next century, New York State operated the Kings Park State Hospital. The surrounding community, which had previously been known as "St. Johnland," adopted the name "Kings Park," which it is still known as today. The state eventually built the hospital into a self-sufficient community that not only grew its own food, but also generated its own heat and electricity, had its own Long Island Rail Road spur, and housed its staff on-site. The campus included an area for tuberculosis patients, as well as a large section devoted to caring for war veterans. At the turn of the century, the hospital had grown to 2,697 patients and 454 staff workers, making it larger than the nearby town of Smithtown.

As the population increased, the hospital grew, building high rises to house the patients. It began to use the new therapies such as lobotomies, electro-shock, and insulin shock. By 1950, psychiatric drugs became the treatment of choice. Reaching its peak population of 9,000-plus patients in 1954, the hospital became quite overcrowded like so many other state-run mental hospitals at that time.

The 1970s introduced deinstitutionalization, and the hospital administration rapidly discharged patients to community-based housing. Many patients wound up living on the streets. By 1996, most of the hospital patients were gone, and the remaining ones were transferred to two buildings on the former Kings Park campus. The dozens of abandoned buildings that made up the center have been closed for over a decade. Closed to patients, anyway, but many ghosts have continued to check in.

The dilapidated, desolated structures may appear to be abandoned, but an amazing network of tunnels links all the buildings to the powerhouse. Given the spooky atmosphere and the thousands of mentally ill patients, you can easily imagine ghosts walking the dimly lit dank tunnels. Two ghostly tunnel walkers are Marie, a seventeen-year-old girl who died while undergoing electric shock, and a man who was said to be brutally beaten and left in small underground room for several days. Visitors to the center have seen misty forms and dim lights flickering; they have heard loud banging and screaming voices; they have felt cold spots and absolute terror. Ghosts also hover near a mass gravesite, located in the northern area of the center. There, the specters chase the living away in an attempt to warn them of the dangers here.

Kings Park
Long Island, New York

The Three Ghosts

Historic buildings are non-renewable resources that cannot be replicated once they have succumbed to fire, vandalism, or the wrecker's ball. They link us to the past, subtly providing us with a sense of personal, and even national identity. Often our ghosts create a link to the past.

The Seneca Falls Historical Society is housed in an 1855 Victorian mansion with a long and varied history. Originally built in 1823, it was a one-room wooden house. Circa 1855, Edward Mynderse, son of the early land developer Colonel Wilhelmus Mynderse, erected a two-story brick structure in the Italianate style on the site. He had a ten-acre estate with carriage house, tool shed, vineyard, garden, and orchard.

In 1875, the Mynderse family sold it to Mrs. Leroy Partridge, who began extensive remodeling and updating that changed the two-story dwelling into the three-story, twenty-three-room, Queen Anne style home that stands today. She had many architectural and decorative details added, including painted and stained glass windows, gas lights, carved fireplaces, and the entire third floor. In 1890, the Norman Becker family purchased the house and raised six children within its walls. The Beckers lived there until 1961, when the Historical Society bought the building.

Three ghosts haunt the lovely old mansion. The first is the ghost of Edward Mynderse, the original owner. A generous man, he also had a bad habit of bankrupting businesses, squandering the family fortune. The staff believes that Edward is the protector of his beloved home: He first appeared in the 1890s after Mrs. Partridge changed the house (from Italianate to Queen Anne style). His ghost is known to stop clocks, turn pictures over so that they face the wall, and lock people out of rooms or the entire building. He has even thrown stuffed animals across rooms and removed tacks from the storm window plastic. Visitors to the museum are informed of the ghost upon visiting.

The second ghost is the Beckers' combination maid and nanny: Mary Merrigan. She often liked to dress the Becker children in costumes and put on plays. When the children were older, she became the family cook. After she appeared naked in Cora Becker's room, she was committed to Williard State Hospital on the doctor's advice. A month later, Cora and her adult daughter were at home one evening when Mary appeared in their living room in a freshly pressed uniform. Instead of taking her to the hospital, they took her up to bed. The next morning she wasn't there, and the hospital was calling to say that she had died the evening before. She has appeared to repairmen, whispered on sound recordings made in the house, and appears occasionally with a costumed child.

The final ghost is of a fifteen-year-old Irish girl, who was hired by the owners but quickly died of tuberculosis. Trapped here, she pines for Ireland: She has been heard crying on the back stairs, which are the ones she would have used.

55 Cayuga Street
Seneca Falls, New York

Cemetery Wasteland

When I was a child and visited my grandmother in Louisville, Kentucky, she always took me to Cave Hill Cemetery so I could "know my relatives." Although I was frightfully bored, I do remember that it was a beautiful cemetery. Not all cemeteries are like that.

Life Magazine is said to have listed Forest Park Cemetery in Brunswick, New York, as one of the Top Ten most haunted places in the United States.

A group of wealthy Troy citizens incorporated Forest Park Cemetery in 1897 in a beautiful 200-acre area. Garnet Douglass Baltimore, the first Afro-American to graduate from Rensselaer Polytechnic Institute (1881) designed the cemetery, but it was never completed because of financial problems. The only structure to be erected was the first above-ground granite Receiving Tomb, large enough to hold 122 corpses during the winter. It featured a domed glass skylight and a copper finial. Burial records indicate that more than 1,000 people have been interred at Forest Park Cemetery.

By the late 1960s, the cemetery had established a reputation as one of the "most haunted" cemeteries in the nation. It occupied only twenty-two acres, although the boundaries were barely visible through the weeds and bramble. Statues were headless, graves were broken or toppled, and the Romanesque Receiving Tomb vandalized. The forgotten grounds were overgrown.

In the 60s, youth found the secluded cemetery an ideal place to party. Perhaps it was the alcohol or other substances, but people began to talk about a headless angel that bled at the neck. More thrill seekers and ghost hunters arrived; some said they saw a large, dark apparition hanging about the tomb; others heard a child's screams. High school and local college students boasted that they had spent a whole night in the haunted cemetery. A popular radio host organized a ghost tour for sixty-five listeners.

Forest Park is a sad commentary on cemeteries. The surrounding area is thick with twisted and misshapen roots and creaking, cracking trees. If you keep going past the front of the cemetery and wander out into the deeper woods, you'll think you've left it. But suddenly, a cluster of gravestones will rise up from the ground along with a couple of creepy headless statues. Some say those statues have been known to bleed. Other stories of Forest Park hauntings include crying babies, dangling corpses, and a vanishing hitchhiker.

An interesting story in the *Troy Record* (October 27, 1996, pp. E1, 4) tells of a couple who "parked" in the cemetery in the 1940s or 50s. The man got out of the car to investigate a strange noise. Somewhat later, the woman heard scraping on the car rooftop. The police arrived at the scene and told her to leave the car and run without looking back. Of course she did, only to see that the scraping sound was coming from her companion's feet scraping against the roof of the car. He was hanging from a tree above.

This graveyard is not as quiet as it appears. *Courtesy of D. Peter Lund*

Another story (although it is told in many towns) is that of the vanishing hitchhiker. According to the same *Troy Record* article, a Troy taxi cab driver said he picked up a young girl dressed in party clothes at Emma Willard School one night. She needed a ride home and directed the cabbie up Pinewoods Avenue, but upon reaching Forest Park Cemetery, the young girl vanished.

Is the cemetery really haunted or is that just an urban legend? Deer leap, and they are in the area. Other wildlife such as Fisher cats or pheasants can make strange screaming-like noises. Do statues really bleed? A certain moss turns red in humid weather when rubbed. Perhaps that could be mistaken for blood.

Today, Forest Park is not so ominous. The dead trees have been cleared away, and the overturned headstones and decapitated statues are the only remainders of its malevolent atmosphere.

Pinewoods Avenue
Brunswick, New York

The Ghosts of the Dakota

"...one of the most perfect apartment houses in the world..."

Opening in 1884 as one of the first luxury apartment buildings in New York City, the Dakota had sixty-five apartments of four to twenty rooms, accessed by staircases and elevators placed in the four corners of the courtyard. It contained a playroom and a gymnasium and had private croquet lawns. It was an instant success. Although the building from the exterior appears to be German because of its stepped dormers, finials, balconies, and balustrades, French residential architecture trends strongly influence its interior.

The building was the culmination of a dream for Edward S. Clark, head of the Singer Sewing Machine Co., who had bought a plot of land between New York City's present W. 72nd and 73rd Streets and 8th and 9th Avenues. Clark commissioned Henry Janeway Hardenbergh as architect, to build a housing development for three different social classes. The development should contain row houses, lower middle-class apartments, and, on the most valuable part of the plot fronting on 8th Avenue, a luxurious apartment house. The latter is known as the Dakota Apartments (1880-1884).

Some say that the reason for its name is that when the Dakota was built in the late 1800s, not many people lived in the Upper West Side of Manhattan, which was considered as remote as the Dakota Territory. What is probably closer to the truth is that Edward Clark liked the names of the new western states and territories. High above the 72nd Street entrance, the figure of a Dakota Indian keeps watch. The Dakota was added to the National Register of Historic Places in 1972, and declared a National Historic Landmark in 1976.

Many celebrities have called the building home over the years, including, Lauren Bacall, Leonard Bernstein, Connie Chung and her husband Maury Povich, Judy Garland, Boris Karloff, John Lennon and Yoko Ono, and Neil Sedaka. Of course, one of the most famous is John Lennon who, along with Boris Karloff, is said to haunt the massive building.

Some say that the Dakota's name is an ironic reference to its distance from the heart of New York City in the late 1800s: It was so far north that people said it could be in the Dakota Territory! For this reason, it was expected to be a financial failure and hence was it dubbed "Clark's Folly." *Courtesy of D. Peter Lund*

John Lennon

Former Beatle John Lennon and his wife, Yoko Ono, began living in the Dakota in 1973. Fascinated by numerology and fate, John Lennon experienced vivid premonitions of his own sudden death by gunshot.

After leaving the Beatles, Lennon enjoyed a successful career on his own with such acclaimed albums as *John Lennon/Plastic Ono Band* and *Imagine,* and iconic songs such as "Give Peace a Chance" and "Imagine." After a self-imposed "retirement" from 1976 to 1980, Lennon reemerged with a comeback album, *Double Fantasy*, which would win the 1981 Grammy Award for Album of the Year. On December 8, 1980, less than one month after the release of the album, Lennon and his wife, Yoko, were just returning to their home in the Dakota. As they neared the entrance, Lennon heard someone call his name. Mark David Chapman, 25, who had been stalking Lennon since October, placed the album that Lennon had autographed for him earlier on to a planter, then fired five shots from a .38 Special, into Lennon's back. Lennon staggered into the building saying, "I'm shot!" Yoko called for help. Two police vehicles arrived in minutes, and one rushed Lennon to Roosevelt Hospital. Lennon died in transit.

Chapman made no attempt to flee. He was arrested standing next to the gun he dropped, reading a copy of *Catcher in the Rye.*

Ironically, just hours before his murder, Lennon told RKO Radio that he felt he could go anywhere in New York City and feel safe. When he was still a Beatle, Lennon was asked how he might die. He replied: "I'll probably be popped off by some loony."

Within minutes, crowds gathered outside the building. They brought flowers and candles, and sang, "Imagine," "In My Life," and "Give Peace a Chance." At least two fans committed suicide when they heard the news.

As of 2009, Ono still has an apartment in the building. On March 26, 1981, the city council adopted legislation designating a 2.5-acre site, stretching from 71st to 74th streets, as Strawberry Fields. It was named after the Lennon/McCartney song "Strawberry Fields Forever." Every year, Ono marks the anniversary of Lennon's death with a now-public pilgrimage to the memorial.

People all over the world are visited by Lennon's ghost, but many insist that they see him in his old apartment building.

Other Ghosts

Apartment #77 was Judy Garland's last residence. Various people have felt the presence of a young boy. Three men who were painting the apartment in 1965 felt they were being watched. One saw a ghost of a boy of about ten dressed in a Buster Brown suit, a style of the early 1900s. A musty odor accompanied the apparition. After the job was done, one of the painters was doing some touch-up work in a large closet. Suddenly, the door slammed, and the light went out. He groped his way off the ladder, propped the door open, and turned the light back on. He felt something grab his arm and put it against the still warm light bulb.

Of course, there are those who insist that they have seen the ghost of Boris Karloff. The long-reigning king of Hollywood horror, he's also said to stalk the halls of the Dakota.

Painters working in the hall saw a girl with long blonde hair and dress of an earlier time bouncing a ball. None of them had seen her before, and she didn't fit descriptions of children who lived there or of any guests. A woman, waiting for a friend in the foyer, saw the same apparition who walked into what she thought was an adjacent room. Later, she discovered it was a closet, and she had seen what others called the "ghost-in-residence."

On the third floor, tenants heard footsteps and other noises in their home. In the dining room, other paranormal phenomena happened. Rugs and chairs slid on their own. One day, when the husband was coming home, he saw, through his living room window, a large crystal chandelier, lights aglow, although none had been there. He thought his wife had it installed as a surprise. When he went into the living room, there was no chandelier, although bolts for one remained.

The Basement Phenomena

The porter summoned one tenant to the cellar because a heavy snow shovel flew off the wall and nearly hit him. He showed him garbage that was thrown about, explaining the bags began to move of their own volition. The tenant was skeptical until a metal bar flew across the room, landing by his feet. He tried to pick it up, but it was too heavy. Other tenants had similar experiences.

An electrician, working in the basement, saw the ghost of a short, long-nosed man with a beard, no mustache, wire-framed glasses and a wig, wearing a frockcoat and high hat. Later, others sighted the same apparition. The description matched that of Edward Clark.

To add to the eeriness, the building was also the setting for Roman Polanski's *Rosemary's Baby*, a 1968 American horror/thriller film based on the bestselling 1967 novel of the same name by Ira Levin.

1 West 72nd Street
New York, New York

The Long Gray Line

Our forefathers placed The United States Military Academy at West Point in the same Hudson River Valley where the headless horseman galloped and Indian tribes wandered. Its gray granite walls conceal several ghosts.

Established in 1802, The United States Military Academy at West Point (also known as West Point) is a four-year coeducational federal service academy located at West Point, New York. The academy sits within the rugged forested Hudson River Valley overlooking the Hudson River; most of the academy's rough-cut stone buildings are NeoGothic. The academy pulses with names from the past: Presidents Ulysses S. Grant and Dwight D. Eisenhower, and the president of the Confederate States of America, Jefferson Davis. It has produced many famous alumni, including Civil War generals Hood, Jackson, Lee, Longstreet, Meade, Sheridan, Sherman, and Stuart; George Armstrong Custer; John J. Pershing; World War II generals Bradley, Clark, MacArthur, Patton, and Stillwell, and Westmoreland. Seventy-four graduates have been awarded the Medal of Honor. The institution is ripe with spirits living by those mystical West Point scripture: "Duty. Honor. Country." Those who have gone before are memorialized in statues, memorials, building names, and street names.

Many ghosts are part of the folklore surrounding West Point. The most famous one, which made national news in October 1972, is a soldier dressed in full Jackson-era uniform first seen in room 4714.

The cadets in that room saw a Civil War ghost, in a Union Army cap, carrying a musket with a bayonet. It hovered over the beds, they said, sucking the warm air out of the room. One by one, the chain-of-command spent a night in that room. One cadet was taking a shower. On leaving the shower, he noticed that his bathrobe was swinging back and forth on the hook. Since the door was closed and the window closed, there could be no breeze causing the robe to move. The temperature dropped about ten degrees.

Two days later, he saw the ghost of soldier in full-dress gray coat, holding a musket. The next night, the room's temperature dropped, and two cadets saw the shadow of a man's torso floating between the floor and ceiling. It remained there for about ten minutes before vanishing. "I don't believe in ghosts myself, but the lads saw something," then Lieutenant Colonel Patrick Dionne told the news crews that flooded the scene.

Then Superintendent Lieutenant General William Knowlton even contacted a pair of supernatural experts to tour the barracks and his own quarters, where strange things had happened. They found that the 47th Division Barracks (old North Barracks) was built in 1938 on a site where a West Point cavalry instructor had burned to death in his house in the 1850s. The continuing visions of a soldier in the cavalry uniform of the mid-1800s created such a distraction on campus that the authorities finally closed the room, reassigning its residents to new quarters. When the room has been reopened, the authorities have found that the phenomena are still present. Room 4714 is now used for storage.

The Jackson-era soldier is not the first ghostly presence to bestir West Point. The ghost of a cantankerous Irish cook named Molly is said to haunt the superintendent's mansion. Molly was Brigadier General Silvanus Thayer's maid in the early 1800s.

Then there's the century-old Morrison House on Professors' Row. When Captain J.B. Bellinger lodged there in the 1920s, two servants slept in the supposedly haunted room. One night they were witnessed running about in their nightgowns and screaming about a ghostly woman. The captain asked a local priest to exorcise the spirit.

Years later, in the 1960s, a young family lived in the house. Their eight-year-old daughter talked about conversing with "a lady." Her parents researched the history of the house. They discovered that in the late 1800s, a young professor and his wife lived there. When the wife contracted a terminal disease, her mother came to care for her. During those hours of caretaking, the professor and his mother-in-law fell in love. The dying woman begged them not to act on their feelings. Once she had died, this early version of a cougar woman married her son-in-law. The heartbroken young wife still haunts the house in her dismay.

LEGENDS

Legends are stories that have been passed down through the generations. They are woven into the fabric of our life, and different areas can hear the same story with variations. Often, they are presented as history, but that may not be necessarily true. New York has many legends.

Sound the Trumpet

In 1626, thirty Dutch families, sponsored by the West India Company, established a settlement called New Amsterdam on the tip of Manhattan Island. The Dutch settlers lived at the lower end of the island between the Hudson and the East Rivers. Beyond the village were hills and woods with small clusters of colonists. Two years later, Director General Peter Minuit arrived in Manhattan and "purchased" Manhattan Island from Native Americans Indians for the amazingly small price of sixty guilders. He also bought Staten Island. He formally established New Amsterdam and consolidated and strengthened Fort Orange up the Hudson River.

Under Dutch rule, New Amsterdam grew to 2,000, although it was little more than a seaport where goods were traded. In 1647, Director General Peter Stuyvesant, often called Old Peg Leg, arrived and took charge. Whenever he wanted to call his people together, say when the Indians were threatening to attack, he would tell his trumpeter, named Anthony Van Corlaer, to blow his trumpet.

Now Anthony knew how to direct air through the center of his pursed lips so fast that his lips buzzed. When he placed his lips on that shallow, cup-shaped mouthpiece, his trumpet would let out a sound so penetrating that people thought the earth and mountains would be transported into the heavens and dissolved into dust. Yes, big old Anthony with his large red nose could hold his breath longer and blow out his breath stronger than anyone else in New Amsterdam.

One night, Stuyvesant learned that the English fleet was coming to attack New Amsterdam. "That will not happen," he announced. "If I have to stand at the cannons on the rickety wooden walls until both my good leg and my silver inlaid wooden peg are shot away, we will defend our city." He told old Anthony, "Go out into the villages on the island and along the river and blow your trumpet stronger than you've ever blown it before. Summon all good men to come help defeat these thieving British robbers who plan to steal our city from the Netherlands."

Anthony hastily kissed his beautiful blonde Dutch girlfriend goodbye, telling her, "You listen, and you will hear my trumpet chasing away those British pirates from our island. I will blow it so loud that it will be heard in heaven and hell."

"But Anthony it is so cold out there. You will freeze."

"Never mind the cold. Old Peg Leg needs me."

Sobbing quietly, she handed him his trumpet and his trusty stone jug, and off he went to signal the colonists. Blowing his trumpet, he traveled the island that cold day. By nightfall, he was at the tip of Manhattan Island, facing the tidewater creek, which connects the Harlem and Hudson Rivers. Overhead charcoal clouds threatened rain; the sky was a menacing purple. The whitecaps on the creek showed their teeth. Pulling his belt tight, yanking his hat down, and shivering, Anthony called out for the ferryman, but no ferryman came. He paced up and down, he shouted, he even blew his trumpet, but only the cold chill wind answered him. Lightning cracked overhead, but no ferryman came. Anthony looked at the creek, took a drink from his trusty jug filled with good Dutch gin and decided he would swim across that creek in spite of the devil *(in spurt den devil).* So he decided to swim the creek in the dark, despite its uncertain currents, with the thundering rain pouring down on him and lightning crackling overhead.

He dove into the water, his gleaming trumpet held high and began to cross the creek. Now the ferrymen might not have heard Anthony calling for them, but the devil had, and Anthony offended him. Who was this upstart Dutchman with the big red nose to boast that he could swim across that creek in spite of the devil? There was no way that the Devil was going to let this man with his big red nose cross that creek. When Anthony was well into the middle of the creek, the Devil caught him by the leg. Anthony pulled out his trumpet and blew a terrific blast, louder than the wind, fiercer than the thunder, sharper than the lightning bolt. It startled the Devil so much that he let go of Anthony's leg. But then the Devil thought, "Am I going to let this Dutch upstart with that big red nose beat me?" So he grabbed him again and began pulling on his leg. Anthony fought back, twisting and turning, trying to avoid the Devil's long bony fingers, but slowly he sank below the waves, never to be seen again.

And that is how the English captured the Dutch fort in New Amsterdam without a fight.

For many years after this, folks living at the northern tip of Manhattan claimed they could hear Anthony's trumpet blowing louder than the wind on nights when it stormed. To this day, the creek is known as Spuyten Duyvil Creek. And as we all know, the English assumed control of New Amsterdam, which they called Manhattan.

Author's Note: Spuyten Duyvil Creek was filled in during the late nineteenth century. The name Spuyten Duyvil currently refers to the southernmost section of Riverdale, below West 232nd Street.

Vampire Corpse

Oneida, New York, takes its name from the Oneida Indians, some of whom live in the municipal area. The Oneida Indian Nation was one of the few members of the Iroquois Confederation to ally with the Revolutionaries in the American Revolution. It still claims a few acres of territory that have never been owned by white men. Their literature is rich with stories.

The Indians were all traveling to a great meeting. Some went by horse, some went by wagon, and some went on foot. Of course, those who walked were exhausted. One couple with a crying child walked all day. When night came, they collapsed in an empty dirt-floored lodge. The husband woke up in the early morning before the sun had risen and heard crunching on the shelf above him. To his horror, he realized that his child was gone. He knew that there were vampires in the region. Probably one had eaten his child!

If he wasn't careful, the vampires would eat him and his wife. He poked his wife and in whispers told her that they had to leave for their own safety. Then in his regular voice, he loudly told her to go outside and make them their morning meal. That way the vampire wouldn't be suspicious of their actions, he thought. She gathered up her clothes and went outside to wait for her husband.

About noon, he said loudly, "I wonder what has happened to my wife. I will go outside and see." He went outside and found her hiding near the cabin, and they began to run as fast as they could. They ran all night; their feet were bleeding and sore. Behind them, they could hear the terrible cry of the vampire. Finally, his wife was so tired that she fell. Her husband told her to lie under a stump of an old tree and use its leaves to camouflage herself.

The husband continued and finally reached the great gathering. People were eating, talking, and dancing. When he got the crowd's attention, he told them about how he had heard the vampire eating his child. A group went back with him to the lodge. Just as the sun rose, they found a corpse with a bloody mouth.

Skulls abound in our history. *Courtesy of D. Peter Lund*

The Galloping Hessian of the Hollow

Many countries and states tell the story of the Headless Horseman, but the American author Washington Irving made the Headless Horseman world renown in his short story, "The Legend of Sleepy Hollow." If you see the Headless Horseman, you run as fast you can, heading for water. Legend tells of a dark shadowy figure that rides a large black stallion. Supposedly, the horseman will disappear if you get on a bridge over rocks and water. This retelling of the legend must be included in a book of New York State ghost stories.

Once upon a time, there was a tranquil valley known as Sleepy Hollow. A brook ran through it; woodpeckers pecked in its trees; squirrels foraged for nuts. The residents of the valley had everything they needed: food, fuel, a school, and a doctor's care. In the long winter evenings, neighbors would gather by someone's fireside, the men would sip some whiskey, and they would tell stories and sing a few songs. The story they told most frequently was the one about the Headless Horseman, who was said to be the ghost of a Hessian trooper riding a large stallion.

During the American War for Independence, George III made a deal with Fredrick II and hired Hessian mercenaries from Hessn-Kassel (the land of Grimm's fairy tales) to fight for the British. The British often hired Germans and other nationalities to do their fighting. During the Revolution, Hessians generally remained in their own units with their own officers. The Hessian trooper, who is integral to our story, was said to have died nearby. Somehow, in the chaos of the battle, the cannonball carried away his head when he was shot. The villagers buried his decapitated body in the churchyard, even though he was the enemy, because they were good God-fearing folks.

About five years after the Revolution and when the Americans were in charge of their own country, the local people began to see the headless Hessian riding on a large stallion in the moonlit gloom. One old man, who didn't believe in ghosts, told of meeting the headless horseman one dark night. The horseman, he said, made him climb up behind him. They rode over bushes, hills, and swamps. Another said, "When he reached the bridge, the horseman suddenly turned into a skeleton and sprang away over the treetops."

An old woman listening to him nodded, "Ghosts and evil spirits don't cross running water."

"When it is dark and the only light comes from your lantern, you see all sorts of things you don't want to see on your path," added another. "One night I swore I saw a light rising from the graveyard and then a white misty figure burst forth..." he gulped. "I ran as fast as I could for the bridge."

One man coming home late one moonless night swore he heard the sound of hoof beats and the crack of a whip on the road behind him. Another saw the horseman in his dashing cape riding around the cemetery; a third saw him riding along the banks of the brook. The villagers said that he was in search of his head. One foolhardy youth collected several large pumpkins and put them on the Hessian's grave, but still people said they saw the ghost riding through the night.

Some people wondered whether they ought to stop going out after sunset. One or two insisted that not even a church meeting or prayer group could get them to venture forth. They said when they came home after work, they blocked their doors. They draped their windows. They kept fires lit in the fireplace should the specter decided to come in through the chimney.

Now the schoolmaster in this town was Ichabod Crane. As you might imagine, with a name like that, he had a tall lanky body, long thin arms, and big feet. His head was a small thing resting on his long skinny neck with its prominent Adam's apple. Although he was not very prepossessing, he had been raised well and knew enough to offer to help the farmers with their chores. He would cut felled trees into lengths, drive the herds to pasture, reap the hay, and pick the apples. In turn, the farmer would ask him to come for supper, and Ichabod would enjoy a hearty farm meal of ham, slaw, preserved peaches, and homemade fruit pie. Later, he would share a pipe with the farmer and his sons and flirt with the farmer's daughters. Sometimes the family and he would sit around the warm fireside and tell stories.

Ichabod particularly liked tales of the imagination, reveling in stories of haunts, whether it were haunted bridges or houses. He enjoyed tales of ghosts, goblins, and of the headless horseman, or Galloping Hessian of the Hollow, as the villagers sometimes called him. He had been seen several times of late, riding about the area and was said to tether his horse among the graves in the churchyard. In turn, Ichabod would tell stories of witches and warlocks, vampires, and trolls.

When it was time for Ichabod to leave a family's warm cozy hearth, he would regret that he had listened to those tales of the supernatural. He took forever to say his farewells, and once he was on the path every stick that snapped, every cold breeze, and every new shadow caused him to jump with fear. All the stories he had heard began to haunt his journey home. Then he would promise himself that never again would he listen to these stories of the supernatural but, of course, he did.

Ichabod was pleasant to everyone, and he always flirted with the girls, but the one he wanted was rosy-cheeked Katrina van Tassel, whose father was the richest farmer in the area. His meadows were lush with crops; his orchard had prolific fruit trees, and his cattle were sleek and strong. A marriage with the buxom Katrina, van Tassel's only child, would make Ichabod a wealthy man. Katrina lifted her eyes to him, tossed her hair about, and smiled winningly. Sometimes she would stand on her tiptoes so that her lips were at his ear and he could feel her breath upon his cheek. When her intended, Brom Bones, saw her acting this way, he would grit his teeth in rage, although he didn't really think that Katrina was seriously interested in the gawky schoolteacher.

Brom was Ichabod's opposite. Strong and muscular, he wasn't well read but he knew how to ride a horse. He was always ready to come up with a practical joke or a prank that would make everyone laugh. He would slap people on the back, letting out whoops of laughter at someone's expense.

One winter night, a most joyous party occurred at the van Tassel's house. The table was groaning with hams, turkeys, pickled beets, roasted turnips, cabbage slaw, and several varieties of cake from plum to seed cake and Ichabod's favorite – Indian pudding. People danced, drank, laughed, and told ghost stories.

When Ichabod reluctantly left the warm fireside to journey home, the night seemed darker than ever. The owl shrieked, the trees creaked, and the moon disappeared behind a dark cloud. The ground was so soggy that it squelched with each step of his horse. The only sound was the constant moan of the wind on the distant hilltops. Even birdsong was notable by its absence. Once he was inside the woods, its shadows closed around him, and the silence became ominous. Branches obstructed his path, and pine needles prickled his cheek. He felt the panic rising within him. He felt certain that he was being pursued. Was that his breath rasping or the thrash of foliage as his stalker gained ground?

Suddenly, Ichabod heard a horrible neighing and the sound of a great horse galloping behind him. He felt his fear rising up his spine and over the back of his head. A horrible cold fright came over him, and he found himself gasping for breath. Spurring his horse onward, he quickened his own pace. All was quiet for several minutes, and then he heard the ponderous *clump clump* of hooves and a rider on a large black stallion pulled alongside him.

"Hello," said Ichabod.

The other rider didn't answer.

"I'm just coming home from the van Tassel's. Were you there?"

Again, no answer. The night grew darker and darker; the stars seemed to fade into the sky and driving clouds hid the moon. The only sound was that of hoof-falls and Ichabod's rapidly beating heart. Ichabod whipped his horse frantically; he had to go faster. The stallion's enormous hoofs thudded along side. The other rider rode besides him, still not speaking. The road was a patch of darkness except for the horses' eyes. Then the moon came out from behind a cloud, and Ichabod could see the leaves of a big tree quivering in the night wind. The hoof-falls of the two horses thudded. Suddenly, Ichabod could see his companion silhouetted against the moon. He appeared gigantic, wrapped in a cloak, but he had no head! Instead, it was tied to the pommel of his saddle! Ichabod whipped his horse into a frenzied gallop, but his companion rode right besides him. On they galloped, through the village of Sleepy Hollow, Ichabod Crane and the headless horseman right behind him.

"If I can just reach that bridge," thought Ichabod, "I am safe." Just then he heard the hoof-falls of the black stallion close behind him; he even fancied that he felt the stallion's hot breath. Another snap of the whip, and his horse was upon the bridge. He thundered over the resounding planks; he was on the opposite side. Ichabod glanced behind him and saw his companion throwing his head at him. Although Ichabod tried to dodge it, the hideous object hit him, tumbling him headlong into the dust. The next day, the villagers found Ichabod's hat and a shattered pumpkin. He never appeared again.

Within two months, a smiling Brom Bones married a giggling happy Katrina.

The Village of Sleepy Hollow is 25 miles North of Manhattan.

Haunted Cedar Knoll

In a remote section in Pelham Bay Park, a knoll lies between the rocky shoreline and a densely wooded area. For generations, stories have been told about this knoll, which lies near the Parish of Christ the Redeemer across from what is known as the Shore Road. Known as Haunted Cedar Knoll, the archeologists have explored it and discovered many arrowheads. There were so many that they believed that arrowheads were actually manufactured here.

But arrowheads are not why stories are told about this knoll. Rather, the knoll is believed to be the site of a fierce battle between the marauding Matinecocks from Long Island and the Siwanoy who inhabited this area. The latter, a band of Algonquin-speaking people, were defeated and allegedly decapitated. Since that fateful conflict, people have reported seeing Indians carrying their heads in their hands. And stories are told about moonlit nights in the area when, if you are very careful, you may be able to see many headless Indians dancing on the summit of the knoll while holding their heads in their hands.

Author's note: On August 20, 1643, the Siwanoy massacred the dissident Anne Hutchinson and six of her children in this area.

The Polly Cooper Shawl

In New York, the Oneidas contributed greatly to the birth of the American nation. Oneidas played a key role in the Battles of Oriskany and Saratoga in 1777. They certainly aided Washington's army at Valley Forge and made many sacrifices for the American cause.

The Polly Cooper shawl at the Shako:wi Cultural Center is one of the greatest relics of the Oneida people. During the winter of 1777-78, Chief Skenandoah organized a gift of corn to be used to feed George Washington's starving military forces in Valley Forge. A group of Oneidas transported the corn by foot more than 400 miles from their home in Central New York to Valley Forge. Polly Cooper traveled with them. She remained in the valley to help the soldiers and to teach them how to prepare the corn.

Since she would not accept cash payment for her part in the Revolutionary War, the officers' wives invited Polly to take a walk downtown with them. While they gazed at the shops' windows and talked about what they wanted, Polly saw a black shawl on display that attracted her. When the women returned to their homes, they told their husbands about the shawl that Polly liked. The US Congress is said to have appropriated money to purchase the shawl, which was given to Polly Cooper for her services as a cook for the officers of the Continental Army. Later during the War of 1812, she served again as a cook in the American cause.

According to the memoirs of Chief William Honyost Rockwell (1870 – 1960), who had heard the stories from his family members, whenever Polly had time between her hours of cooking duty, she would roll up her sleeves and take two pails of water, one container in each hand, and walk to the battlefield. There, she would slack the soldiers' thirst on both sides of the firing line. The shawl is still owned by members of the Oneida Nation, descendants of Polly Cooper.

Shako:wi Cultural Center
5 Territory Road
Oneida, New York

Captain Kidd's Treasure

Although many pirate stories talk about buried treasure, finding such treasure is rare according to researchers. The treasure more often ended up at the bottom of the sea or in the pockets of the shop owners in the pirate's favorite ports, such as Port Royal, Jamaica, where they squandered their booty on demon rum.

Throughout the nineteenth century, the Hudson Valley was rife with stories that the fearsome Captain Kidd had buried his treasure somewhere in its rugged forested landscape. One story says that in the town of Hughsonville near Poughkeepsie, the ninety-year-old Mrs. Talmadge dreamed about Captain Kidd's pot of gold on three successive nights. Now, the way the story is told, Mrs. Talmadge was a person who people respected. Perhaps they respected her because she had been born on Halloween just before midnight or perhaps it was because she had been born with a caul or maybe it was because she was ninety years old and she read tea leaves...

Mrs. Talmadge told her family that she saw a very tall man in her dream. He towered well above her, but, of course, given her ninety years on earth, she had shrunk. She insisted the tall man was Captain Kidd – not that she had ever seen the captain or a picture of him – but she knew. And when Mrs. Talmadge said she knew, everyone believed her. She saw this man burying bags of gold at the base of a giant oak tree in a small grove of trees about four miles away. The spot, she said, was "between the folds of the tree that formed two huge roots." She even described the gold coins and their markings – so obviously, she had seen them in her dream. Mrs. Talmadge dreamed this same dream each night. Each morning she repeated it at the breakfast table: the way the tall man looked, the bags of gold, and the shiny gold coins.

Mrs. Talmadge lived with her son William, who was not a rich man but a happy one. His business did well – so well that sometimes he employed two or three other people. He and his wife Cynthia Talmadge were quite content. Just three years ago, they celebrated their golden wedding anniversary, which was a milestone in those days when people did not live as long as they do now. The two of them cared for their family and friends, helped their neighbors, and worked hard. When evening came, they looked at each other over the supper table and smiled peacefully. At night, they slept in each other's arms, both gently snoring.

William wondered whether he ought to dig for the treasure, but he was too busy making shoes. Cynthia thought what ease that treasure could bring to their lives, but she had grandchildren to care for, suppers to make, and laundry to be washed. So they shrugged their shoulders, ignored Mrs. Talmadge, and said they were too busy with life to be yearning after treasure that may or may not be there.

Their children did not feel the same way. Eighteen-year-old twins, Matt and Jim wanted to find the treasure. Their grandmother told them, " You go at night, you hear. You have work to do during the day, and you don't want anyone to see you there."

"Yes, Gram," said Matt dutifully.

"And when you get there, you be silent."

"Why?" asked Jim.

Mrs. Talmadge drew herself up. Her eyes glittered like ice. "How many times have I told you that silence is necessary when digging for buried treasure."

"Oh, I thought that was just part of your story."

"Well, it's not." Her eyes snapped with anger.

The moon was very bright when Matt and Jim set out. When they turned into the woods, the moon was reduced to pale shafts of light. Fortunately, they had a lantern, and they found the grove and the giant oak tree.

Working in silence, they began to dig. The only sound was the occasional call of the owl and the noise of their shovels. They dug for about twenty minutes, making a good-size hole, when Jim heard a *thump! thump! thump!* and the ground began to tremble with the noise of someone coming. He looked up and saw a great tall giant standing behind his brother. If he stood up upright, Matt's head would only reach the giant's knees. The giant was so tall that his elbow was level with the treetops. Jim was so scared that his teeth began to chatter and he dropped the shovel. Matt turned and froze when he looked up at the giant. Their grandmother had been right. The treasure was well guarded. Slowly, the arm of the giant rose and motioned them to leave the grove. They ran for their wagon, jumped into it, and shouted "Giddy up." Their horse sensed their fear or perhaps he too knew that something was wrong; he took off in a flash.

The next morning, Matt and Jim went back to the grove. Their shovels lay beside the giant oak. The earth between the oak's spreading roots was smooth as silk. It didn't look like it had ever been touched. The moss was velvety smooth yet they knew this was where they had piled the dirt last night. Dejected, they collected their tools and went home.

That night they visited the local tavern, drank several beers, and told their story. The small group of listeners decided they would have better luck than the two young grandsons of Mrs. Talmadge, but the giant terrorized them, too. Over the years, others tried, but the giant remains guarding the treasure. It has never been found.

The Burning Horse

Pirates have been around for a long time. The Vikings could even be considered pirates since they attacked ships and ports. Many pirates were outlaws, but, thanks to Hollywood, many of us think of pirates as the dashing, well-educated sons of upright families. We view them as the swashbuckling Robin Hoods of the sea, sporting cocked pistols, eye patches, and cutlasses. They know how to swashbuckle, mop the poop deck, use a cat o'nine tails, and – if they must – walk the plank.

Some, like John Hawkins, profited royally from stealing slaves from Portuguese ships off West Africa and selling them illegally all over the Spanish Main. Some, like English-born Blackbeard, chose piracy over unemployment at the end of one of the many European wars. Others were like Stede Bonnet, who had retired from the Army, owned a large property in Barbados, and lived in a fine house with his wife. His neighbors understood that because his wife harassed him so much, he had become unbalanced mentally and had taken to piracy.

Of course, avarice was the great culprit. The great riches of the Spanish Main were what lured so many seafarers into the life of a pirate. From the sixteenth to the eighteenth century, the Spanish fleet would transport great hoards of gold, silver, gems, spices, hardwoods, leather, and other riches from the New World to Spain. Although buccaneers are supposed to have wooden sea chests loaded with gold bullion, pieces of eight, and jewels, their treasure was more often hogsheads of sugar, pewter, silverware, bolts of cloth, and other practical necessities from captured merchant ships. The pirate captain sometimes took the whole ship as a prize and forced the captive crew to join them.

Although we often think of pirates as belonging to the Barbary Coast of Africa, eastern Long Island was well acquainted with pirates. Fishers Island, Gardiners Islands and all the many Long Island coves were fine hiding places for pirates who were ready to raid, rob, and destroy. Governor Peter Stuyvesant had a difficult time keeping Long Island Sound safe for merchants and sailing vessels. He assigned forty men to watch the sound and to give an alarm when they sighted a suspicious vessel, but they too could be misled.

One beautiful day when the skies were clear blue and dotted with puffy cumulus clouds, buffeted by a northeastern breeze, a small sailing vessel sailed out from Pelham Bay. The ship carried a cargo of furs, some passengers, and a beautiful white stallion. The breeze was good, the sun warm, and the passengers enjoyed the sight of the glistening sound and its islands as the ship glided through the waters. Although the passengers were relaxed, the captain kept his eye on the horizon for he knew pirates could suddenly appear from any small cove or behind an island. Just as the sun was sinking, the captain saw a boat approaching them. There was something suspicious about the look of the boat so the captain ordered his sailors to arm themselves, while the passengers gawked in horror. Would they really be under attack by pirates?

The captain took evasive actions, but the other boat drew closer and closer. Soon the passengers could see the pirates standing in the other boat, with their cutlasses in their teeth. Their tight-fitting clothes were brightly colored; one had a patch over an eye. Another was brandishing a large sword. The pirates called to the captain to surrender. One woman began to weep. Her husband drew her close, shielding her eyes.

The captain pulled his gun and shot at one pirate. Screaming and yelling, the pirates pulled their ship abreast to the vessel, throwing grappling hooks over the rail, and swarmed aboard.

The crew and the passengers tried to defend themselves, but they were swiftly killed. One shrieking woman was thrown overboard. The pirates quickly removed the cargo and ripped the jewelry off the dying passengers. The pirate captain yelled at his crew, "Tie that horse to the mast and set the ship on fire." Once that was done, the pirates boarded their own craft, leaving the burning vessel behind them with nothing alive on it but the shrieking white horse.

The red-hot flames crackled around the vessel, black smoke spread over the water, and the horse reared in panic, but ever so slowly, the dead passengers and sailors arose from the deck and continued as they had before the arrival of the pirates. The wind flapped in the burning sails, the flames crackled, ashes billowed from the vessel, but no one spoke. The only sound was the neighing frantic horse. Sparks flew from its hoofs as it kicked against the flames. Meanwhile, the passengers continued to sit and admire the ocean and its waves, and the sailors worked on the sails and rigs in silence.

On stormy nights when wild northeasters rage over Long Island sound, the golden burning craft with the frantic horse can be seen from shore, bobbing, lurching, and gliding through the water. On foggy mornings, it is barely visible through the haze.

The burning ship and horse have been seen at Hell Gate and Gardiners Island, and even beyond.

The Golden Comb

Sometimes the dead return to resume their simple everyday lives again.

Once upon a time, an Irish couple in Albany, who had a short but happy courtship, married with great plans for the future. John and Sheila saw themselves in a cute little cottage with four cute little children and a dog and a cat. They happily bickered about what they should name their children. They had already named their small brown and white dog, Max.

One day, they went for a picnic in the great forest. They took Max and packed some lemonade for Sheila and beer for John and ham and cheese sandwiches. They found a lovely peaceful dell near a rushing brook. John went off to gather some pine needles to sit on while Sheila set up the picnic on the red and white checked cloth. While he was gone, a large branch fell, striking Sheila on the head, killing her instantly. When John returned, he thought she was asleep until he realized she was dead. Heartbroken, the young widower could barely sleep in his misery. Previously with his lovely Sheila at his side, his life was golden; now all that was gone.

John spent days lying on his couch, grieving with Max besides him. One night he felt a gentle repeated caressing of his hair, one of Sheila's loving habits. The next night he caught a sudden movement in the kitchen window. A distinct human form walked back and forth outside. Max whined and wagged his tail.

The third night, he saw a glowing light outside his window. When he got out of bed, he saw a young woman with her back towards him. She was standing in the moonlight combing her long brown hair with a golden comb. "From the back, she looks just like Sheila," he said to Max, "but I need to see her face to be sure. After all, she could be a banshee, who according to my grandmother's tales, were always combing their hair." Max wagged his tail. Finally, the woman turned around. She was his Sheila! John gasped, and she disappeared.

Throughout the next day, he wondered about what he had seen. Certainly his granny had often talked about seeing the spirits of the departed, but he didn't know anyone else who had seen them. Perhaps it was a dream? Maybe he was going crazy. "If it was a dream," he said to Max, "she will not come again. But if she does come again, I will grab at the comb. For if the comb in my possession when morning comes, then it is no dream at all but my own dear Sheila who hasn't crossed over." Max watched him intently.

That night John didn't go to sleep, but stood hour by hour at the window waiting, hoping that Sheila would appear. When midnight came, a bright light appeared at the window again. His beloved Sheila stood just outside his window, combing her hair over and over with the gold comb. He quietly moved forward, not saying anything. Quickly, he grabbed the gold comb. The light and his Sheila vanished in a blaze. Disgusted, he said to Max, "I wanted Sheila – not a comb." He put the gold comb in a drawer in his chest. She didn't come the next night or the next. She didn't come for the entire week. Each night, dark-eyed with fatigue, he waited at the window. Max sat by his side. The comb remained in a drawer in his chest.

The seventh night, he succumbed to his fatigue. He went to bed with the gold comb held tightly in his hand. At midnight, Max whimpered, and John woke up suddenly, but he wasn't sure what had awakened them. Then he saw a bright light outside. He slowly went over to the window where Sheila stood. She looked at him sadly, "John, I need my comb back."

He slowly opened the drawer. Very carefully, he slid the comb over to her. She smiled gently at him. "Thank you, John."

"I miss you, Sheila."

"And I you." She turned away.

"No," he said, "Don't go."

"But I'm no longer part of this world, and I need to pass over."

"There must be a way that you can come back to me."

She looked down at him and then she began to smile. "I can remain and perhaps come back if you do as exactly as I say without telling anyone."

"Tell me."

The following Friday, the town had a great parade. The shopkeepers, the farmers, the local bands, the scouts, and the cheerleaders all paraded down the street. John didn't watch any of these. He kept waiting for the end of the line, the last horse. Then down the street, just after the biggest band with its blue-suited musicians playing their trumpets, clarinets, and drums came a beautiful white stallion, prancing in the sun. Riding it was his Sheila with her head high and her eyes proud. Just as she had told him to, John waited, crouching low by the roadway. Then when she was abreast of him, he dashed out from the sidewalk and circled her waist with his arms and swung her lightly to earth. Her arms were about his back and her lips pressed to his.

In this way, he rescued her from crossing over, and she stayed with him for a long and happy life. And every night John combed her long brown hair with the gold comb.

The Vengeful Son

Strange lights can appear in haunted houses to puzzle and terrify those who pass by.

The village of Waterford, New York, has several claims to fame. It was incorporated in 1794, making it the oldest incorporated village in the nation or so they say. It is also the home of the Northeast's largest annual tugboat festival and a haunted house.

Around 1900, a young carpenter, his wife, and two children lived in a poor little house on the waterfront. He had tuberculosis, which made it hard for him to keep a job. When he asked his parents for help, they laughed. He begged, but his parents, a mercenary couple, demanded that he sign over to them the title for his home. He refused. They walked away. Two weeks went by, and the cupboard was empty in the poor little house. He went to his parents again. "How about providing groceries for my family? They are your grandchildren after all."

They shook their heads. "You need to sign your house over first, son."

The young man fumed. His children's hungry wails drummed at his ears. His wife became pale and drawn. "Please, honey, sign the paper," she begged. "Our children will die."

Finally, he gave in to them, signing the house over to his parents. Shortly before he succumbed to his disease, he warned his parents, that if they did anything that harmed his wife or children, or if they made life hard for them, he would haunt them for as long as they lived. They pretended they were listening to him, but secretly they were planning their future as rich landlords.

Once their son died, his avaricious parents took possession of the house, dispossessing their young daughter-in-law and their two grandchildren. They planned to rent the house, but it was a miserable little house with holes in the roof and walls and poor plumbing. It required so many repairs that they couldn't rent it – and they certainly didn't plan to live in the worn-down hovel. So they locked the doors and closed the shutters to wait for a tenant.

No tenant ever came because soon the neighbors began to see lights going on and off at night. Although no one was in the house, the lights danced all night. One neighbor chuckled, "You know before he died the former owner told his parents he would come back to haunt them."

"Well, he certainly is doing that."

"That house is haunted by those lights, I'd say. I'd never rent it."

"Pretty spooky." Soon people began walking on the other side of the street; the neighborhood children called it the haunted house, and no one ever rented it.

Ultimately, the house collapsed, and the mercenary parents had to pay to drag the remains away.

Shelter for the Night

Several tell the tale of the man and his wife who were driving home in a carriage to Troy from a trip to her parents in New England. As they approached Spiegletown, the sun set. "Oh my dear," said Ruth. "We must find a room for the night."

"Of course. But I'm not sure where we will find an inn."

"It certainly looks deserted here." The horse clomped along as the twilight set in. The woods looked black in the fading evening light. "Wait a minute, Robert. I see a light through those trees."

"So do I. Let's turn in there. "He turned the horse into the wagon path that twisted beneath the trees up a hill. The path may have been dirt, but it was well cared for: There were no ruts or obstructions. The birds were settling for the night as they traveled down the path. Although the night was enveloping them, they could see from the lights ahead that the cottage was quite small.

At the doorway stood an old man and his wife in their long flannel nightclothes. "Come in, come in," they said when they learned that the couple needed a place to spend the night.

"Tie up your horse in the barn behind," said the old man. Robert went around back with the horse.

"Come on in," said the old woman to Ruth. "Are you hungry? I can put on a pot of tea. And I just made some gingerbread cake this afternoon."

Ruth felt her stomach gurgle with delight. They had been driving for a long time, but she politely said, "Oh, you shouldn't go to any trouble," although she certainly liked the idea of having some freshly brewed tea and warm spicy gingerbread.

"Don't be silly, my dear. You need some refreshment, I think. Aren't you in the family way?"

Ruth gasped. "How did you know?"

"You just had that look about you." The old woman patted her shoulder. "Now you come in and sit down."

Ruth stepped into the small cottage. It had a large red and white quilt hanging on one wall, a pine rocker in a corner, a large cast iron stove, and a big purring cat lying on a comfortable-looking coach.

Robert entered. "Look," he said to the elderly couple. "We don't want to put you out, but my wife is tired and we do need a bed for the night. Can we pay you?"

"Don't be silly," said the old man. "You are our guest for the night. We don't have much company these days, and it is nice for us to have you two stop by. Now, sit yourself down at our table and eat some of my wife's famous gingerbread."

"Well, then we thank you. You certainly are wonderful to invite us into your home." They finished their cake and tea and went to bed in a sturdy four-poster bed covered with quilts. Before they went to sleep, Ruth whispered to Robert, "Can we leave them some money? She was so nice!" They fell asleep, arms around each other, breath on each other's face, heads touching.

Next morning, Robert and Ruth awoke at the sound of the first birdcall. They quietly left the house, leaving a shiny half dollar on the kitchen table. They hitched up their horse and set forth as the birds began to sing. They traveled for about thirty minutes before they stopped for breakfast at a little inn in Spiegletown. As the restaurant owner served them, Robert said, "Who's that nice couple who lives on the dirt road about three miles back?"

The restaurant owner looked startled. "Where did you say that house was?" he asked. Robert described the location in detail.

"You must be mistaken," said the restaurant owner. "A fire destroyed that house three years ago and killed the owners. They were a nice elderly couple. She made good gingerbread as I recall."

"No way," Robert declared. "They were alive and well last night. We ate some mighty fine gingerbread!"

After a brief discussion, the restaurant owner hung the closed sign across the restaurant door, and the three of them drove the carriage back the way they came. When they turned into the muddy lane, Ruth noticed the great ditches on either side. The path was bumpy and overgrown with weeds. At one point, Robert had to get out and push a fallen tree out of the horse's path. They climbed the hill to the crest, where they found the remains of a cellar hole, one partially remaining wall, and a few burnt timbers on top of a table.

" This is weird, " said Robert. "We didn't see this before."

Ruth suddenly gasped in horror. "Look, Robert, look." She pointed at the burnt timbers. There on top of the halfway-concealed table was a shiny half dollar.

Hudson Valley is often compared to Germany's Rhine River Valley because of its natural beauty. The area was the home of many wealthy New York tycoons such as John D, Rockefeller and William Vanderbilt. Once Erie Canal was open, the area became an important industrial center. During the mid twentieth century, many of its industrial towns began to decline. *Courtesy of D. Peter Lund*

'Tis the Gift to Be Simple

The Shakers, or United Society of Believers in Christ's Second Appearing, are one of the most successful of the many communal societies established in America in the late eighteenth and early nineteenth centuries. Their founder, Mother Ann Lee, an English mill worker, emigrated from Manchester, England, in 1774. She and other early Shakers established communities connected by their shared faith and a commitment to celibacy, common property, gender equality, pacifism, and separation from the world. They were committed to creating Heaven on earth.

By the 1860s, some 6,000 Shakers were living in eighteen communities in New England, New York, Ohio, Kentucky, and Indiana. Today, the sect is virtually extinct, since Mother Ann regarded sex as a device of the devil, and Shaker "brothers" and "sisters" lived in separate dormitories. Their only mutual recreation was prayer meetings, at which they sang hymns and "shook" together in frenzied dances. Their shaking and trembling at their worship services was the way they rid themselves of evil...hence the name.

Mother Ann Lee admonished her followers to "Put your hands to work and your hearts to God." The results can be seen in their craftsmanship, which is world renown for its elegant simplicity. Credited with a multitude of innovations, they invented a flat broom, an apple parer, a circular saw and many other labor-saving devices, based on their belief in simplicity, purity, and perfection. Even today, architects and designers attempt to replicate their sparse yet elegant furniture and utensils.

Well known for their medicinal herb and garden seed industries, Shaker communities cultivated herbs, raised produce for seed, and processed herbs and plants (e.g., belladonna, hops, native ginger, chicory, dandelions, wormseed, black cohosh, basil, poppies, and pennyroyal) for sale to the "World." Supposedly, seed packets began with them!

Hancock Shaker Village is nestled on twelve hundred acres of farm, woodland, and meadow. *Courtesy of D. Peter Lund*

The Hancock Shaker Village in Pittsfield, Massachusetts, is a popular tourist attraction in the Berkshires. Visitors have the unique opportunity of dropping back in time by a century or two and touring this graceful renovated village with its 1,200 acres of farm, woodland, and pasture. Heritage breeds of animals such as shorthorn cattle, Merino sheep, and silver-laced Wyandotte and Dominique chickens roam the fields. Two heirloom vegetable gardens contain plant varieties on Shaker seed lists from the 1830s and 1890s, respectively.

The buildings hold a major collection of Shaker furniture and household items. "Wherever you go, you feel that you are beyond the realm of hurry," wrote one visitor in 1977. "There is no restlessness, or fret of business, or anxiety; it is as if the work was done, and it was one eternal afternoon." (*Time Magazine*, 1969)

About six miles west of Pittsfield, Massachusetts, in New Lebanon, New York, is Mount Lebanon Shaker Village, a former major force in the agricultural, commercial, and institutional activities of its day. It contained over 6,000 acres and 100 buildings. With the coming of the Industrial Revolution, and naturally declining population of the celibate community, the Shaker membership dwindled, and communities consolidated and closed. In 1947, the remaining property of the North Family was sold into private hands, and the remaining Shakers relocated from there to nearby Hancock Shaker Village in 1947. Seventy-two acres and approximately forty original Shaker buildings were declared a National Historic Landmark District in 1965. The Shaker Museum and Library, whose preeminent collection is currently housed on a non-Shaker site nearby, purchased the North Family Site of Mount Lebanon in 2004 and is revising a master plan for relocating to the landmark property, thus repatriating many of the Shaker objects and artifacts back to the place where they were created.

In the meantime, Darrow School, a private secondary school, and the Sufis, a spiritual group, used some of the former Shaker buildings. Generations of Darrow students have claimed to have seen Shaker ghosts. One popular apparition is a woman wearing an apron and bonnet peering out the windows of the Carriage House. Of course, she is always seen at night. The Sufis, who moved into another part of Shaker buildings in 1974, are said to be aware of the ghosts.

Every Shaker society has a place for meeting in the open air, usually at some little distance from their village. There they assemble at least twice in the year. Usually, on these hills there is a building with two apartments: one for the sisters, and the other for the brothers. A fountain acts as the center for their marches, dances, songs, and play.

As the story goes, the Shaker community was living under the threat of eternal hellfire. As their elders told them, the Lord had raised their foes high against them. Sisters in other communities, who had been known for their staunch devoutness, had become covered in darkness and lust, eloping with corrupt freethinkers. Brothers were not abstaining from lust and uncleanness, but enjoying card games and carnal pleasures. Obviously, it was difficult to be celibate and devoted to the Shaker virtues of simplicity, purity, and perfection, when the rest of the world chose to remain in a state of corruption. The adherents of the anti-Christian teachers had broken the laws, disobeyed the statutes, and violated the eternal covenant in their folly and blindness. Surely, Sodom and Gomorrah never went so deep in sin. The world had become a frightening place.

Their Elder Gabriel Patton was most distressed about these evil influences on his flock. With eyes burning, he exhorted them to be aware of the Devil's influence. "This powerful, unseen evil spirit is a master of lies and deception. He has blinded you to God's truth. Satan has dominated people from the time of Adam and Eve. We want what we shouldn't have; we long for sinful things. If you unlock that door so temptation can get in, you are sinning. Let God in instead. Come to Zion and wander no more."

One member of the community was Sister Martha Tomlinson, who joined the community after her husband and child had died. She came from the eastern part of the state. Initially, she had seemed quite content with her decision to accept the Shaker way of life. During the last several months, however, she had been deeply depressed, often weeping throughout the night. Several of the sisters were concerned that she no longer gave her superiors the customary reverence and showed the requisite obedience to their ways. Consequently, they subjected her to a multitude of penances, such as compelling her not only to kneel, but also to prostrate herself before Eldress Mary. Even that humiliation was without effect.

Elder Patton said, "Like John said, the whole world is under the control of the evil one. The world values those things that are contrary to God's will." Elder Patton was afraid that his people would succumb to the worldly ways of the unbelievers.

He cautioned, "The devil has successfully turned other sisters and brothers away from God. Be careful, my brothers and sisters. He is trying to tempt you. The devil is all around us. Satan is attacking our community, and his demons are fighting to control, influence, entice, and dominate us. They devise cunning schemes against us and conspire to make us weak. Be strong."

Believing that Satan and his forces were assembling, he told the assembled community that true believers would defeat the Devil. "Prepare ye, my sisters and brothers, for the final battle. With the help of the Lord, we shall strike down the evil one."

On the appointed day for the battle, every able-bodied brother and sister in the Shaker community assembled. Only Sister Tomlinson, who was in bed with a fever, was absent. In the early dawn, they gathered in the meetinghouse, where the elders stood at one end of the hall, and the eldresses at the other end. Two brothers approached together and knelt down before the elders, and two sisters approached the eldresses. The elders and eldresses pantomimed throwing something towards the kneeling brothers and sisters. It is said that two little angels standing close by received the suits of invisible armor from the elders and clothed the faithful subjects in these suits, which had the power to shield the truly faithful from the Devil. And so the Shakers, who were pacifists in the temporal world, were clothed with the glorious apparel of righteousness. In this way, they prepared to battle the Devil, the Power of Darkness.

Dressed in invisible armor, each one carried a Bible in one hand and the sword of the Spirit in the other. Singing one of their early ballad hymns, "Mother," they marched shoulder to shoulder, finding pleasure in their strength and unity.

At the top of the mount, they began to narrow the circle around the Devil. As they drew their circle tighter and tighter, a vile odor filled the air. The Shakers recognized the stench: They knew it was the smell of sulfur and brimstone. When their ring became so tight that they could see their reflection in each other's eyes, they heard the sounds of the Devil: horrendous howls, harsh curses, and the sibilant preternatural hissing of that serpent of evil. Elder Patton commanded them to advance still further, so that the Devil would be prevented from escaping. With a bestial shriek, the Devil died.

The Shakers celebrated their formidable victory with fervent singing, dancing, whirling, and shaking. The young sisters turned so swiftly that the air gathering under their skirts raised them, exposing their red petticoats and other underclothes. Sometimes in their enthusiasm one or two would fall prostrate upon the floor. In spite of their victory, they later found that the devil had, in fact, left his mark on their community by claiming one last victim.... Martha Tomlinson, who had ended her life.

Darrow Road, off Route 20
New Lebanon, New York

Peeping Tom

In beautiful Steuben County, a man took his girl friend home early evening and began the walk back to his house. The ancient trees creaked as the breeze softly blew. The birds sang their final calls. After he passed several farmhouses, he approached a decrepit house, which was generally believed to be haunted. Although he knew that it wasn't really haunted, he still believed the old stories of demons and spirits, phantoms, and strange clawed creatures.

To keep up his spirits, he began to whistle. Sepia and gray fragments of memory, images, and faces floated into his mind and then melted away. He heard the distant bird calls rather like the sound of music after the note has ended. A breath of wind lifted the leaves of the large beech tree in front of the windows of the house. He blinked as the desolate mansion seemingly rushed to meet him, blurred at first than somehow brighter than before.

In the moonlight, he saw that the old place looked different from the way he remembered it. The grass was mowed, the shutters hung primly on their hinges rather than hanging askew. He heard music, laughter, and the tinkle of glasses. He could smell roast beef in the air and fresh homemade bread.

When he saw the light within, he decided to move closer and peek in. Creeping quietly over the grass, he saw that the house was decorated with garlands, flowers, and greens. Victorian trumpet vases stacked on silver candy compotes were centerpieces on mirrored plateaus. The buffet was filled with sweets and savories, including a fruit and nut topiary.

A woman dressed in purple satin and bedecked with diamonds sat down at the piano and began to play. Feet began to tap; eyes sparkled. Two of the young men rolled back the big Oriental rug so everyone could dance on the polished oak floor. A pretty young blond clapped her hands together. The fire crackled and snapped in the large granite fireplace. The Peeping Tom moved closer. The night murmured around him, conjuring up the ancient spirits of the woods.

Suddenly, there was a high, piercing agonized scream. Then the lights went out, and he was staring through the broken window of the deserted haunted house he knew from before.

He ran home. Several days later, he mentioned what he had seen to his girlfriend. She nodded somberly. "You're not surprised?" he asked. "You don't think I'm crazy?"

"Oh no, what you saw was a party that occurred many years ago – a party that ended in a woman's murder. Each year, at the time of the tragedy, they all return to the house and reenact the murder."

The Ghosts of Devil's Hole

Seventeen miles (27 km) north-northwest of Buffalo, New York, the Niagara Falls are the most powerful waterfall in North America. Renowned for their beauty, the falls are a valuable source of hydroelectric power and a major attraction to tourists and honeymoon couples. Most of us know about the happy, romantic, heart-shaped tub-for-two image of Niagara Falls, but few have heard about the dark side.

The Seneca Indians believed Niagara Falls to be the home of deities known as the Great Spirit of Thunder Waters, He-No the Thunderer, and Lewlawala, the Maid of the Mist. The area around the Three Sisters Islands was reportedly the location of their sacrifices to the Great Spirit. Legend says that when the wind rises the visitors to the area can hear strange whispers and the screams and wailing of the thousands of suicides.

The eastern bank of the Niagara River from the falls to Lake Ontario has been the scene of countless suicides. Each year, between twenty and twenty-five sad souls are said to take that final jump at Niagara Falls, which is second only to San Francisco's Golden Gate Bridge as the nation's top suicide destination. In the *Niagara Falls Reporter* (May 27, 2008), Paul Gromosiak wrote that 2,780 known suicides occurred in the falls between 1856 and 1995, although he admitted that the actual number is probably much higher, as many of the bodies are never recovered.

One popular jumping-off point is located at the rapids at the twenty-foot-deep cave known as Devil's Hole. The Senecas believed the Evil One, a giant snake, lived there. A beautiful walkway leads down from Devil's Hole State Park into the wooded gorge, but, be forewarned, Devil's Hole is a dangerous place.

On September 14, 1763, at least 300 Senecas, Ottawas, and Ojibwas attacked a supply train along the Niagara Falls portage. Two companies sent from Fort Niagara to rescue the supply train were also defeated. More than seventy soldiers and teamsters were killed in these skirmishes. The English called it the "Devil's Hole Massacre," the deadliest engagement for British soldiers during the war.

In 1892, construction began on a scenic attraction, the Great Gorge Trolley, which ran from Niagara Falls to Lewiston along the banks of the Niagara River. Between 1895 and 1935, trolley cars that were powered by overhead electric lines carried 17,000 thrill-seeking passengers a day. Up to ten cars ran at a time, carrying enthralled visitors just a few feet away from the whirlpool rapids, Devil's Hole, the Narrows, and the Giant Rock. The evil spirits associated with Devil's Hole plagued the Great Gorge Trolley.

On September 6, 1901, United States President, William McKinley, with his wife and entourage rode on the Great Gorge Route. Hours later, President McKinley was assassinated at the Pan Am Exhibition in Buffalo.

On February 12, 1906, the Canadian shop and car barn burned to the ground. On March 12, 1907, an avalanche of ice just north of the Whirlpool Bridge killed a conductor and eight passengers. In 1910, two trolley cars crashed head-on at the upper end of the Whirlpool Rapids. In 1913, a garbage chute located under the Great Gorge rail bed exploded, showering a passing trolley with tons of semi liquid sewage. On July 15, 1915, a trolley car carrying a Sunday school group from Toronto derailed, rolled over and crashed into a tree, killing and injuring people. On July 1, 1917, twelve tourists died, and twenty-four tourists were injured when a trolley filled with passengers derailed and plunged into the Niagara River at the upper end of the Whirlpool Rapids.

Eventually, the Great Gorge Trolley was shut down, but still Devil's Hole is thought to be one unluckiest places in New York State. Many think the ghosts of those who died still lurk within its dark, clammy depths. People report hearing the sound of moans and the wails of dying men. Some scoff at the ghost stories, but no one likes to be there for long.

Robert Moses Parkway
1 mile north of Whirlpool State Park
Niagara Falls, New York

Tall, Dark, and Hairy

Although it is just a small town, Whitehall, New York, has been famous for many centuries. As early as 1690, the French were using this location, then known as Skenesborough, as a staging ground for incursions against their opponents. Because of its strategic location on one of two main transportation corridors through the wilderness, the region was the scene of much activity through the French and Indian War. In 1776, Benedict Arnold (yes, the Revolutionary War general and traitor) built a fleet here, making it the birthplace of the American Navy.

And then there's Bigfoot.

Throughout the centuries, Whitehall, New York, has developed a major reputation for so-called sightings of Bigfoot-like creatures, extending from the Algonquin and Iroquois era to 2006 newspaper reports. This small town on the Vermont border at the south end of Lake Champlain between Lake Champlain and Lake George is considered such a "hotbed" of eastern North American Bigfoot activity that legal action has been taken.

Bigfoot Sightings

The Algonquin told stories about the windigo or "giant cannibalistic man" who roamed the countryside. The Iroquois also told tales about powerfully strong flesh-eating giants. Champlain in his ship's log wrote how numerous Indian tribes in the St. Lawrence region had told strange stories of a giant, hairy man-beast they called "the Gougou." Champlain wrote that so many of the tribes recounted such stories that he believed there must be some truth to the tales.

During the last century, teenagers, police officers, school teachers, and others have reported seeing a large, hairy, eight-foot creature that stands on two feet, frequently exudes a bad meat-like odor, and often leaves enormous ape-like footprints at the scene. It is verbal; according to some witnesses, it sounds like a hysterical woman.

In 1976, three teens saw a seven-to-eight-foot hairy creature in a field. It made a sound, they said, that was a cross between a woman screaming and a pig squealing. They reported the creature to the police. Checking out their report, several police officers reported sighting a large creature, "at least seven or eight feet tall and a good three hundred pounds. It had red eyes."

The Bigfoot Field Researchers Organization believes the town is one of the hottest spots in the country when it comes to finding Bigfoot. Members say alleged sightings in the area have been multiplying and have been constant for more than thirty years.

According to the organization, in January 1989, (Class A) hikers found footprints and saw a ten-foot tall creature outside a home. The 2008 "Monster Quest" reported numerous sightings of a large, hairy, ape-like creature on both sides of Lake Champlain. On an August evening, two fishermen spotted what they thought was a black bear. Suddenly the "bear" stood up and walked off, leaving the men shaken. One of the witnesses said it stood seven feet tall and had dark-brown hair. "Its face was hairy yet fleshy around the upper cheeks. Its eyes were dark in color but clearly visible and had a brightness about them." The creature stared at the two terrified fishermen for ten seconds before ducking its head and fleeing into the woods.

No Hunting or Trapping

If you're planning a Bigfoot hunting expedition in Whitehall, you're out of luck as the village board approved a resolution that makes it illegal to hunt the elusive creature. On January 29, 2004, Paul Bartholomew, a local researcher, proposed, "a resolution that would make it illegal to shoot Bigfoot." He commented that the idea was mostly symbolic, adding "it would be a step toward bringing notoriety and tourists to the area." On February 5, 2004, the Whitehall village board approved the resolution that makes it illegal to hunt Bigfoot in Whitehall, New York.

The Lady of the Lake

With its occasional sandy beach and lightly wooded shoreline, Lake Ronkonkoma appears to be quite placid. The lake, which was formed by the melting of a glacier, was thought to be bottomless until divers discovered that it was only sixty-five feet deep. For years, however, it has been the source of ominous Native American legends on Long Island! Most of these are based on the belief that the lake is haunted.

Before the white men came to the area, a tribe of Setauket Sachem Indians lived in what is now Sayville. The tribe had a beautiful Princess called Ronkonkoma.

Now beautiful princesses often act as catalysts for various legends, which frequently revolve around unrequited love and supernatural revenge. In this case, the theme remains the same: An Indian princess "many moons ago" died in this lake and vowed revenge. Her spirit, which remains within its water to this day, has lured many a young man to its murky bottom.

The forms of the tale vary slightly, usually in the method of death for the princess (accident vs. suicide), where her body was found (in the lake, in a Connecticut river, in the Long Island Sound) and the identity of the male lover (European settler, childhood sweetheart, warrior from a rival tribe). However, they all end with one young man drowning each year.

Legend 1

The Sachems were one of four tribes bordering the lake in the mid 1600s, a time that witnessed the increased presence of settlers on Long Island. The beautiful princess fell in love with the woodcutter Hugh Birdsall, who lived in a log cabin on the banks of nearby Connetquot River. On moonlit nights, Ronkonkoma would steal away into the forest and make her way to Birdsall's cabin, where she would watch him from the forest.

One summer night, a sleepless Birdsall paced back and forth in front of his cabin. Suddenly, the princess, clad in colored glass beads, stood before him in the moonlight. Birdsall fell in love with Ronkonkoma immediately.

Her father, however, forbade the marriage and refused to let his daughter ever see Birdsall again.

For many years, the two lovers continued to communicate. Everyday, the princess would write a note about her desire and longing on a strip of birch bark and then paddle her canoe to the middle of the lake and gently float the note. Everyday, for all those years, Birdsall would await those notes.

One day Ronkonkoma, bursting with pain of lost love and solitude, sent a mysterious message to her lover, saying only that she would join him in the morn. As dawn broke, Birdsall waited faithfully by the lakeside and witnessed a canoe rushing towards him as if guided by magical hands. Inside was his princess, nestled amidst boughs of pine, with a knife through her heart.

Birdsall's tears fell into the lake. Without hesitation, he leaped into the canoe and cradled her lifeless body. They both sank into their watery grave.

Ever since, her ghost rises once a year and pulls a young man down to the lake's depths.

Legend 2

Princess Ronkonkoma was in love with an Indian prince from the Poospatuck tribe on the other side of Brown's River. She was forbidden to visit there. One day, they snuck off together to Lake Ronkonkoma and took their canoe to a romantic spot after dark to make love. The spirits did not approve of this, as people on opposite sides of the river should not mix. So the boat sunk, and their bodies fell forever and ever down into the bottomless lake. So every year, the angry Princess kills two lovers and pulls their souls to the bottom of the lake. And every year, at least one young couple dies.

Legend 3

Princess Ronkonkoma fell deeply in love with a young man of her tribe. She eagerly awaited her upcoming wedding day as she dreamed of their life together. Unfortunately, one week before they were wed, a white settler from the nearby town of Ronkonkoma murdered her love. The Princess was distraught; life could not exist without her love. The man who killed her lover would never pay for his crime. Her family tried to help her but they didn't know what to do. They tried to speak to her and begged her to calm down, which only made her cry that much more. Frightened by her grief, they left her alone by the fire the night before her intended marriage. She rose and dressed in the gown she'd made for her wedding and walked silently to the shores of the lake. When she peered into the lake, she saw her love looking up at her from just below the water's surface. His spirit called to her. She called back to him, swearing they would be together always, and that together, they would get justice. Then she rowed herself out to the center of the lake, tied rocks to her own ankles, and threw herself into the lake.

Her saddened family could not recover her body from the lake. Some say that while her tormented soul was dying, the Princess vowed to avenge the tragic death of her lover. Once every year, she appears on the shore, a beautiful ethereal Princess, dressed and waiting for her wedding day. It is said on the day she appears, she lures a man to accompany her to the never-ending bottom of the lake in vengeance for her lost happiness. And every year, at least one male dies swimming in Lake Ronkonkoma and hardly ever is his body found.

Legend 4

"The Troubled Spirit of the Lake" tells the story of a broken-hearted maiden who was going to be sacrificed to appease a god, Manitou. Consequently, she could not marry her love. So she tied weights around her ankles, rowed to the middle of the lake, and slipped over the side. Her lover dove into lake after her, and their bodies then turned up in the Connecticut River weeks later. The Native Americans believe her spirit haunts the lake and causes "whirlpools, waves, moaning sounds, and other mysterious events."

Local residents confirm that drowning incidents are frequent at the lake. The ghost of the Indian princess is said to dwell in the depths of the lake, and each year, according to some, she drags down a least one young man to be her lover in death. The authorities and media back their claim that there is at least one drowning per year and almost all are males. Interestingly, only a few women have drowned in the lake. People have also reported hearing intense heartbreaking sobbing coming from every direction. A fog is said to hang over the lake along with strange lights. Cold fingers grab swimmers who begin to swim too far out.

Old Fishing Friends

Two friends co-owned a hunting camp, not far from the lovely town of St. Regis Falls. Every fall, they would go there for a few days' hunting, drinking, and swapping stories. One day, only Ed returned. He said that his friend, Barry, had disappeared. A search party returned with him to look for Barry, but an early snowfall made the trip north impossible.

The New York State Police thought there was something suspicious about the case. Ed didn't look them in the eye when asked questions, and he became flustered, stuttering and backtracking. But the corpse had not been found so the case was dismissed.

In the spring, Barry was found lying at the base of a tree with a broken skull. Still, the police couldn't prove foul play. Besides his body, they found his rifle, but his hunting knife was missing.

The next fall, Ed went back to his camp with a new companion. The first night they arrived, the newcomer went to sleep early. He was awakened by Ed screaming, "Don't do it! Don't do it!" When the newcomer pulled himself out of his bunk and found his flashlight, he discovered Ed dead in his chair with a hunting knife stuck through his neck.

Later, the fingerprint expert for the New York State Police found that the fingerprint on the knife belonged to – Barry!

A Loch Ness Monster in the United States

"There is also a great abundance of many species of fish. Amongst others there is one called by the natives Chaousarou, which is of various lengths; but the largest of them, as these tribes have told me, are from eight to ten feet long. I have seen some five feet long, which were as big as my thigh, and had a head as large as my two fists, with a snout two feet and a half long, and a double row of very sharp, dangerous teeth. Its body has a good deal the shape of the pike; but it is protected by scales of a silvery gray colour and so strong that a dagger could not pierce them."

– Samuel de Champlain, Volume 2, Chapter IX

Today, historians believe Champlain saw a garfish, a class that includes lake sturgeon, which are still living there today.

Does New York State have a Loch Ness Monster? People from St. Regis Falls, New York, believe it does. That town celebrates his existence with their Annual Champ Day celebration, the first Saturday in August. At the southern entrance to Port Henry, a Champ Sightings Board lists the names of people who have seen the lake monster. A full-size replica of Champ is situated in the middle of the village. Champ has been featured on popular TV shows such as *Today, Unsolved Mysteries,* and Discovery Channel. Of course, Champ, like Loch Ness, could be just a legend guaranteed to bring the tourists.

Increasing sightings and the continuing "theories" of so-called monster hunters have resulted in keychains, mugs, T-shirts, and even "Champburgers" (seafood patties on sesame-seed buns) along with great, revenue-generating media attention. Such endeavors have made Champ the best-known lake monster in the United States.

Both Lake Champlain, which borders New York and Vermont, and Loch Ness in Scotland are freshwater lakes dug by glaciers over 10,000 years ago. With a maximum depth of 400 feet, Lake Champlain can easily provide Champ with plenty of hiding room. One researcher has calculated that either Champ is 10,000 years old or a breeding colony of 30 or more of the monsters, yet no remains have washed up since 1926, when a large decaying carcass was found on the shore.

Like the Loch Ness monster, Champ has a thick body, is fifteen to fifty feet long, depending on whom you talk to, and has four fins, a long tail, and a long sinuous neck. That description is very similar to a plesiosaur (a marine reptile extinct for more than sixty-five million years). It behaves like a nocturnal creature, being seen most often at twilight and night.

Over the years, at least 300 sightings of Champ have been reported No one knows who first reported it, but Native American tribes who lived in the vicinity of the lake confirm that they believed a "horned serpent" lived in the lake. Both the Abenaki and Iroquois tribes living on Lake Champlain had their own legends of a creature in the lake – the Abenaki called the creature Tatoskok. In 1819, in Bulwagga Bay, Port Henry, a railroad crew reported to have spotted a "head of an enormous serpent sticking out of the water and approaching them from the opposite shore." Around the time of this sighting, nearby farmers claimed to have been losing livestock and seeing drag marks leading to the shore. In 1873, the *New York Times* reported that a railroad crew had seen the head of an "enormous serpent" in Lake Champlain, with bright silvery scales that glistened in the sun. Everyone retreated at that point.

In July 1873, the Clinton County Sheriff reported seeing an "enormous snake or water serpent; he calculated it was twenty-five to thirty-five feet long. In August, the steamship *W.B. Eddy* ran into Champ, which nearly capsized the ship, according to the tourists on board. That same year P. T. Barnum, an American showman known for hoaxes and for the circus that became the Ringling Bros. and Barnum & Bailey Circus, offered a reward of $50,000 for the "hide of the great Champlain serpent to add to my mammoth World's Fair Show."

In 1977, the most famous sighting occurred. As Anthony Mansi went back to the car, Sandra Mansi kept an eye on her children playing in the lake. A "turbulence" in the water made her look more closely, and a huge creature with a small head, long neck, and humped back surfaced. She took an Instamatic photograph.

In 1984, the captain of the excursion boat, *Spirit of Ethan Allen*, saw a dark object about twenty-five feet long and three feet wide that paralleled the boat. It swam parallel with the boat with its three or four humps setting up a wake, until an approaching speedboat caused it to dive. Between seventy and eighty-six passengers were aboard. The creature remained for about three minutes.

In 1993, several women were swimming in Button Bay State Park in Ferrisburgh, Vermont. A baby Champ interrupted their peaceful time in the water.

On July 11, 2005, when two men were fishing, they saw what they thought was a log or a railroad tie. When they trolled over to it, they found a living thing with a back that was good three or four meters long and a serpent body.

If you wish to see Champ, you need to watch the lake. Many claim that the friendly beast is scared off by boats and will swim away from any water disturbance. This characteristic shyness makes Champ hard to sight, but obviously many people have. In 1981, Port Henry declares their waters a safe haven for Champ; in 1982 and 1983 both, Vermont and New York passed resolutions protecting Champ. So if you see Champ, don't harm him – just take a good photo and prepare yourself for instant fame.

The Protective Ghost

Some ghosts are very protective ghosts. They keep trying to tell their children how to live their lives the right way.

Once upon a time a very rich man lived in Westchester County. He had done many evil things in his life. He had lied, cheated, stolen, and coveted. He gambled, consorted with prostitutes, and borrowed money from his friends and didn't pay them back. He had not honored his mother or father; he worshipped himself. As he grew older, he realized that he had done all those things that he ought not to have and done none of the things that he should have, but he knew he was too old to change that.

"The one thing that I can do," he said to his wife, "is to set Hamilton, my son and heir, on a better and more moral path."

"Oh, my dear Martin, I'm so glad to hear you say that," she said. "Only you can set him straight. He's already doing all the wrong things."

In his final weeks of his life, Martin spent many hours talking to his son, lecturing to him about changing his way of life. Of course, Martin was bored by these lectures, but he knew that his father was dying and he was an heir so he decided at least he could sit by his side and listen to him. Or at least pretend to. So he sat, nodding where appropriate and saying, "Of course," "I hear you, Dad," and "Right on, sir," when necessary. During Martin's last moments here on earth, he said to Hamilton, "I shall be watching you every minute of every day. If you step over the bounds into mortal sin, I shall return and make you suffer for it." Hamilton nodded solemnly and folded his hands in prayer.

At first, Hamilton behaved admirably; perhaps it was because he knew how serious his father was. He gave up his late nights on the town, his gambling, and the women, and began to concentrate on the family business. He did well. His instructors were surprised at his prowess. His more dissolute friends began to ignore him because he was no longer ready to gamble for high stakes or to go out on the town. His family began to speak to him again. He started talking about what he would do in the future: a job, a wife. ...

The Cathedral Church of St. John the Divine at 1047 Amsterdam Avenue in New York City is said to be the largest Gothic Cathedral in the world. Its thirteen acres of gardens and the marvelous sculptures, including the Fountain of Peace by Greg Wyatt, offer an oasis of quiet in the middle of the bustling city. *Courtesy of D. Peter Lund*

Then his old ways caught up with him again. Towards the end of the first year, Hamilton's financial affairs went from bad to worse. He was in danger of losing everything he owned: house, investments, and his father's entire estate. The only way he could escape these losses was to steal from his company. One day he did.

The next night, he heard a strange sound outside his bedroom door. It was the sound of chains being dragged up and down the hall. When he called for his servants, the noise ceased. The next night, he ordered all the doors and windows to be closed and locked. He decided to stay up all night. Shortly after midnight, he heard the rattle of chains coming closer and closer. He felt a cold draft and chills go up his spine. Turning, he saw a misty figure wrapped in a winding sheet that covered his face. Hamilton knew he had locked his door.

He jumped up from his chair, demanding, "Who are you? How did you get in?" There was no answer. The specter came closer.

"What do you want?" he asked. Still no answer. The specter came closer. The closer the specter came, the more frightened Hamilton became. He shouted again, "Tell me your name!"

The specter still did not reply. So Hamilton picked up his silver letter opener and thrust at the mysterious specter, only to see his blade pass right through its neck. Terrified, he leapt at the figure and unwrapped its face.

Staring at him was his father. He screamed for the servants, but by the time they arrived, he had fainted.

The following night, he asked the police to send a detail to watch the estate, although he didn't really believe that a simple patrol officer could capture the elusive midnight chain rattler. He brought one of his largest dogs into the room with him, ordered all the doors and windows to be locked, and sat down by the fireplace. Suddenly, the dog moaned. Then, it went to the window, saliva dripping from its mouth, staring outside. A cold breeze blew the curtains open. Hamilton saw his father wrapped in his winding sheet standing just inside the window. When the servants found him the next morning, he was unconscious; the dog was dead.

The servants took Hamilton to the hospital, where he told them what had happened the night before. The doctors and other professionals smiled and nodded, but he could tell that no one believed him. The physicians told him that there was nothing wrong with him at all, but Hamilton insisted on staying within the safety of the hospital Since he had contributed to the hospital foundation, they let him stay. On the third night, the nurses prepared him for bed, shutting the window, pulling down the shades, and giving him an extra blanket. The nurses said good night and left him. Twenty minutes later, they heard a hair-raising scream coming from his room. Three nurses rushed into to quiet him, but he already lay dead on the floor beneath the open window.

Alice at the Bar

It couldn't have happened anywhere but in little old New York.
– O'Henry

You know my mother always told me never to pick up girls at bars, but when I saw her on that dark wet night, I thought she's the girl for me. She was sitting alone, nursing a beer, but her eyes sparkled when she looked over at me, so I said to my friend, Frank, "Come on, I want to meet her." So we moved over, introduced ourselves.

She said with a big smile, "Sit."

I bought her a beer and ordered another for Frank and myself. We talked and laughed and laughed and talked. When the bartender shouted "last drink," I asked her if she wanted a ride home. She said, "Oh, I'm all right. I'll walk."

But the night was cold, the rain had begun, and she didn't even have a coat. I said, "Come on. We won't hurt you." By then, we were standing next to my car, and she was shivering. I took off my old black leather jacket and put it around her shoulders, "Don't be silly now. Get in." So she got in the car, and I asked her address.

"30 Oak Street," I began to drive. As I approached Oak Street, she said, "Stop."

I put my foot on the brake, thinking maybe I had run over something, but she just wanted me to let her out.

"Here on this deserted block.? Are you nuts? "

"Look," she said, "I'm only a block from home, and my mother will have a fit if she discovers that I let two strange men take me home. You know how mothers are." Well, I certainly do know how mothers are, so I agreed and she got out. "Thank you. I hope to see you again."

It wasn't until later when we were almost home that I realized she had gone off with my old leather jacket. Frank pointed out that we knew where she lived and where she hung out too, so I could get it back.

A few days later, Frank and I decided that we would like to see her again. Maybe she would have a girl friend so we wouldn't be competing. We went to the bar where we had met her, but they hadn't seen her. So then we went to 30 Oak, where she said she lived. Number 30 was one of many brick houses with a double flight of stairs up. I knocked at the door, and an older woman bundled up in a navy blue sweater came out.

"Yes?" she said, looking up to me.

"Does Alice live here?"

"No, Alice hasn't lived here for years."

Frank interjected, "But she said she lived here."

She drew herself up proudly. "Are you doubting me young man?"

"No, but... you see we met this girl named Alice the other night and she said she lived here and we'd like to see her again."

"Maybe take her out, " I added.

"Hmm," she said. "You wait here. "She went off and came back with a photograph. "Is this the girl you're taking about?"

"Yes. That is. So you *do* know her?"

"Yes, I did. That's my daughter Alice, and she has been dead for these past five years. "

We were stunned. What do you say to something like that? So we went home, but Alice remained with us. She had been so alive, how could she be dead? So I said to Frank, "Why don't we go to her grave, and see if she really is there."

"Okay," he said. And we went to the cemetery and found the grave of Alice Adams, dead at age twenty-one, beloved daughter of Ernest and Margaret Fitzpatrick.

Frank looked at me. "How do we really know that she's in there?"

"What do you mean?"

"Well what if they just put up this gravestone, but she isn't there. What if we really saw her? How could we both have seen the same ghost?"

"You mean you think we should dig up the grave?" Frank doesn't believe anything unless he sees it with his own eyes.

"Yep, that's what I mean."

So two nights later, we got our shovels and went into the cemetery at night, which is really spooky, and started to dig. The first few feet of dirt were frozen solid, and it broke up in chunks with the smaller pieces sharp as glass. Eventually, our shovels hit the coffin's edge. We slid the wooden box out carefully.

The moon was bright as I pried off the top with my shovel and opened the lid of the coffin. Alice was there all right. She was wearing my black leather jacket.

LORE

In ages past, our old ones were the storytellers. Folks sat around the supper table and shared stories with each other. Their tales were part of our heritage. They were ones we all know – that we have grown up with. In the case of some of these retold stories, American painters and authors have added to their allure through their art.

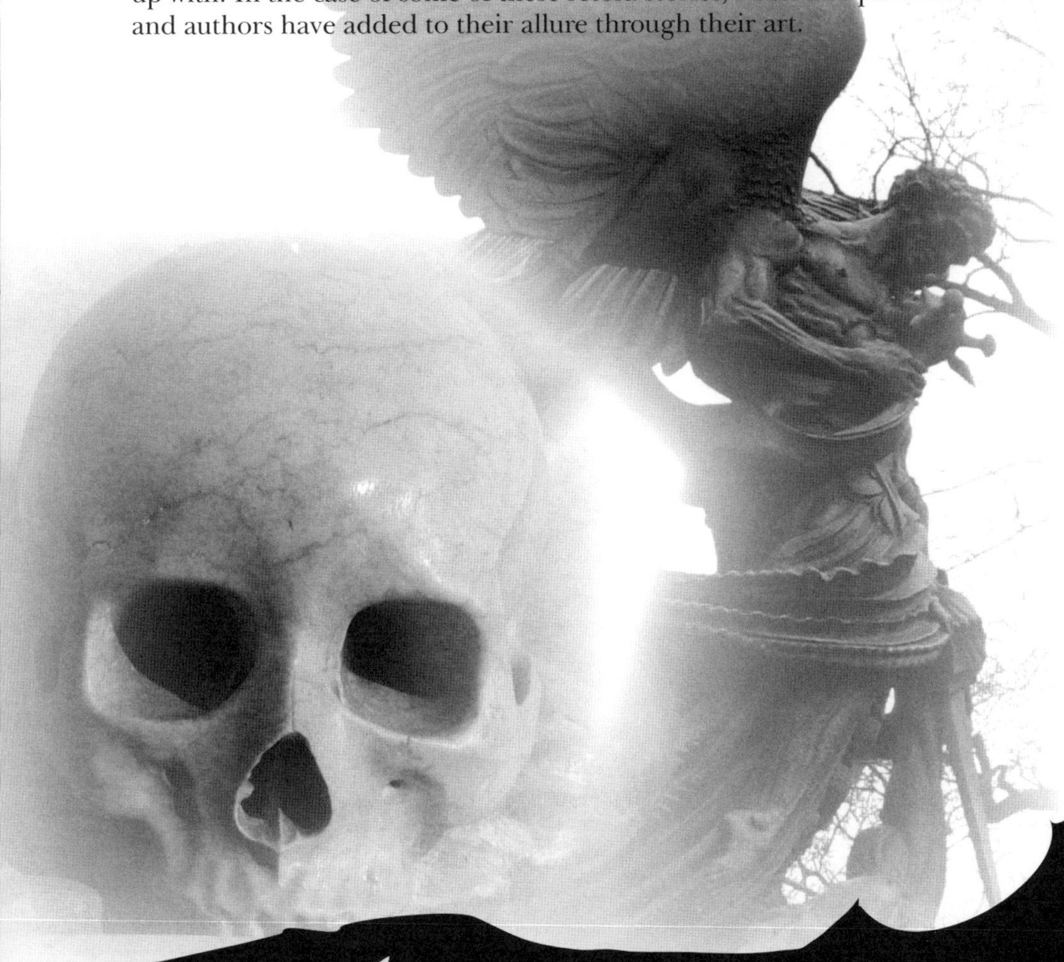

Jane McCrae

The awful circumstances of her death made Jane McCrea one of the best-known American women of the eighteenth century. Some claim her death greatly aided the American cause and contributed to the defeat of British General Burgoyne's army at Saratoga on October 17, 1777 – one of the most decisive victories in the history of the United States. Her story became a part of American folklore when John Vanderlyn painted "The Death of Jane McCrea," in 1804. James Fenimore Cooper described similar events in his novel, *The Last of the Mohicans.* (1826)

The daughter of a scholarly Presbyterian clergyman, Jane or Jenny McCrea was an orphan living with her brother, John McCrea, on a newly cleared farm on the Hudson River, below Glens Falls and near Fort Edward. She is said to have been most attractive, charming, and well liked.

Jane was in love with David Jones, who is described as a brave, generous young man. She and David had grown up together in New Jersey; his family had followed hers to New York State. Their love for each other had one major problem: She lived with her brother John, who was a Patriot and a colonel in the Colonial army. Her fiancé, David Jones was a Royalist, who was a lieutenant in Burgoyne's army. Jane was caught between her brother's patriotism and her lover's Toryism.

General Burgoyne commanded the British forces charged with gaining control of Lake Champlain and the Hudson River valley. His forces consisted of British soldiers and Native American allies, whom he relied on to create havoc and terrorize the Colonial forces. The summer of 1777, General Burgoyne planned to rendezvous at Albany with another British army under General Howe coming north from New York City and a smaller force that would come down the Mohawk River valley under Barry St. Leger. When Burgoyne, with his fierce Indian allies, was in the proximity of Fort Edward, David was able to communicate with Jane. The couple decided that her brother would never approve of their relationship and that as soon as Burgoyne advanced she and the other settlers would be sent for safety to Albany. Consequently, they decided she should join David and be married at once.

David arranged that Jane should travel to join him at Ticonderoga, where the officers' wives accompanying the expedition would arrange their wedding. She would be safe with him, he thought. Leaving her brother's home, Jane reached the village surrounding Fort Edward, where she stayed with an old Loyalist friend, Mrs. McNeil. Most other settlers in the area had already fled for Albany.

The morning of July 27, 1777, some of Burgoyne's Native American allies returning from a raid descended on the village. As a Huron party approached Mrs. McNeil's house, the two women ran for the cellar, but the Hurons dragged them out by their hair. They mounted Jane on a horse, but forced Sara to walk because she "was too heavy to be lifted on the horse easily." The two groups split up.

When news of the abduction reached the British camp, David sent another Indian patrol to escort his fiancé safely to the encampment.

The story of Jane's death has several versions, but we know she was scalped. One theory is that a Huron named Le Loup had captured Jane; he wanted ransom money in return for the young woman. When the escort group sent by David met Le Loup, they proceeded to guide Jane toward the British camp. Le Loup, angry at the interference and afraid of losing the ransom money, attempted to retake his captive. An argument ensued at the base of a "Giant Pine," at the roots of which flowed a spring of water. During the skirmish, Jane fell from her horse, and Le Loup scalped her.

The other theory is that members of a Colonial militia fired at the fighting Indians, accidentally killing Jane. The Hurons then scalped her.

Someone brought David her scalp, and he identified the long blond hair as hers. Mrs. McNeil was returned to the British camp. David remained at his post. Despite the loud clamoring for justice, General Burgoyne refused to punish the Hurons, knowing he would lose his Native American allies if he did. His decision enraged local Americans, and many men now enlisted in the struggle against the British. The incident continued to be used as propaganda against the English throughout the war.

The Giant Pine was felled in 1853, and made into canes and curio boxes, which were sold as souvenirs at the New York Crystal Palace Exposition. The spring, known as the "Jane McCrea Spring," still runs.

Jane's remains have been moved three times. In 1822, she was moved to State Street Cemetery in the village of Fort Edward, where her remains were placed atop the brick vault of Sara McNeil (who had passed away naturally in 1799 at the age of seventy-seven). In 1852, Jane's body was exhumed again and moved to the newly created Union Cemetery in Fort Edward.

Jane McCrae's ghost is rumored to haunt the house known as the Jane McCrae House, which was built back in the Revolutionary War period in the town of Fort Edward. One story says that Jane was scalped in a closet in this house, but researchers have disproved this. Nevertheless, people who have lived in the house experience lights turning on and off and footsteps in the attic. People feel a cool draft in the closet where Jane was supposedly scalped. Sometimes, screams can be heard from it during the night. No one actually sees Jane's ghost so we don't know if she remains scalped in the spirit world!

Union Cemetery
Route 4
Fort Edward, New York

The Britannia at 527 West 110 Street, New York City, is decorated with limestone gargoyles much to the delight of passers-by. *Courtesy of D. Peter Lund*

After defeating the British in the Siege of Boston in March 1776, General George Washington, Commander-in-Chief of the Continental Army, brought his forces to New York. There he established his defenses and waited for the British to attack. In July, British General William Howe and his forces landed on Staten Island, where they increased their total force to 32,000 troops. With the British fleet in control of Long Island Sound, Washington knew he would have difficulty in holding the city. When the British won the Battle of Brooklyn, Washington's troops began to retreat. On September 15, 1776, General William Howe landed in Kip's Bay, which is on the east side of Manhattan, intending to capture the American General Israel Putnam and his rear guard of 4,000 men. Mary Murray knew that Putnam was in imminent danger. His troops were rapidly retreating within a mile of her Long Island home and heading up the Hudson to the high ground of Harlem Heights and Fort Washington and that the British troops were almost double those of Putnam's army.

War on Murray Hill

Mary Lindley Murray was married to one of the richest New York merchants in the days of the Revolution. They owned a beautiful summer home at what is now known as 5th Avenue and 37th Street – or as Murray Hill. An avenue of mixed trees leading from the Boston Post Road approached the large square house; porches on three sides commanded views of the East River over Kip's Bay.

One of the most successful and wealthiest merchants in the city, Mr. Murray, a Quaker, believed in the British cause. Mrs. Murray and her beautiful daughters were solid supporters of the Revolutionary effort. Life around the dining room table in this house had to be most interesting.

One hot day in September, General Washington visited Mrs. Murray and her daughters. Luckily, Mr. Murray was away on business. General Washington knew how charming she was and how devoted to the Revolutionary cause. "Dear friend," said General Washington, " I need your help."

"Of course. What can I do for you, General?"

"My forces under General Putnam need just a few more hours to reach my main army that's on the shores of the Hudson River. Perhaps you can use your wit to detain the enemy."

"But of course," she said. "I will have my servants prepare refreshments." After he left, Mrs. Murray and her daughters saw a group of British officers approaching. Their red coats shone in the sun. The pace of their horses stirring up the dust of the road.

"Look, Mother," said one daughter. "The British are coming."

"They certainly are. We must do our best to keep them entertained so General Putnam and his troops can make their escape."

General Howe, who was a close friend of Mr. Murray, approached. "Hallo there, Mrs. Murray. How are you?"

"Welcome General. Isn't it a warm day?"

" Indeed, it is." He glanced at the attractive mansion with its lawn and graveled walks and wiped his sweaty brow with his big red hand.

"My house is cool. I have some wonderful cakes. Why don't you and your officers alight and refresh yourselves? "

"I do thank you, Madam, but I must first catch that Putnam and his forces."

"Did thee not hear he has gone? It is too late to catch him. Why don't you come in to my cool dining room – out of the sun – and lunch with me. I have some fine cold meat and freshly caught fish, and my daughters and I have made a tasty cake. "

"That sounds most pleasant. We deserve to take our respite with you and enjoy your company."

The general and his officers dismounted their horses. The daughters curtsied and smiled. "Come, you must taste our good brandy."

The servants quickly set the table with fine china, gleaming decanters of wine, and platters of steamed clams. Howe and his officers ate and drank with great enjoyment. They lingered there for several hours. Finally, they stood to leave.

"We must keep them longer," Mrs. Murray whispered to her eldest daughter. "Gentlemen," she said, "I know you must make your leave, but first you must hear my maid Daisy sing. She has such a lovely voice."

"That would be pleasant."

"I'll fetch more wine and some cold meats and cakes." Mrs. Murray sat back down again. Daisy began to sing, and the men drank more while General Putnam and his 4,000 men slipped away up the Hudson.

Finally, a servant came and whispered to Mrs. Murray, who turned to General Howe and asked him to accompany her. She took him to an upper window and pointed out Putnam's army vanishing in the dim distance. The delay had enabled the Americans to escape. The General nodded grimly, saying, "We will catch him the next time, but this interlude was lovely on a hot September day." As the British soldiers were mounting their horses, a young officer came galloping up. "Sir," he said to General Howe, "Sir, the rebels have escaped – all of them with their leaders. We should have left earlier."

General Howe dismissed him with a wave. "Young man, the fine feast we just had and the company of these lovely ladies are of much greater importance than chasing after that riff-raff mob of rebels. We can catch them anytime." He then bid farewell to Mrs. Murray and her daughters, and the British force rode away.

"My dears," said Mrs. Murray, putting her arms around her daughters. "I am proud of what we accomplished today. General Putnam and his 4,000 men have had plenty of time to join General Washington's army up the Hudson."

"But did General Putnam run away?"

"No, my dear. He who fights and retreats lives to fight another day."

Author's note: Many members of Mrs. Murray's family were Revolutionaries and served in Washington's army. Because of her help and her family members, General Washington did not exile her Royalist husband at the war's end, as was the case for many others who remained loyal to the British king.

The Haunted Tunnel

Few of those many people who crowd the busy streets of downtown Brooklyn know that they are walking or driving through a tunnel that is nearly two hundred years old. Described by Walt Whitman as "dark as the grave, cold, damp and silent," this tunnel had been kept secret for many years – thanks to greed and corruption.

Walt Whitman knew about this 17 feet high, 21 feet wide and 1,611 feet long tunnel. In a column for the *Brooklyn Standard* called "Brooklynania," Whitman wrote:

> *...the old tunnel, that used to lie there under ground, a passage of Acheron-like solemnity and darkness, now all closed and filled up, and soon to be utterly forgotten, with all its reminiscences; of which, however, there will, for a few years yet be many dear ones, to not a few Brooklynites, New Yorkers, and promiscuous crowds besides. For it was here you started to go down the island, in summer...*
>
> – Walt Whitman, "Brooklynania" #36, 1861

Cornelius Vanderbilt, who is better known as Commodore Vanderbilt, made his wealth in railroads and shipping. The director of the Long Island Rail Road, he wished to create a rail/ferry/rail connection from New York to Boston in the mid-nineteenth century. As part of this connection, he had train tracks built on congested Atlantic Avenue in Brooklyn, which was a city bristling with activity in the mid-nineteenth century. In those days, trains had no air brakes and took up to eight city blocks to come to a stop, which meant that if the train engineer wasn't careful a fatal accident could happen. And if a train had an accident, it was no longer on schedule, which bothered the directors.

To avoid this problem, the Long Island Rail Road decided to build a tunnel so the trains could avoid the congestion in downtown Brooklyn. The resulting tunnel, Atlantic Avenue Tunnel, is said to be the very first underground transportation system or the very first subway in the country.

Unlike the Hoosac Tunnel in the Berkshires, only two deaths are associated with the construction of the tunnel. The first was a local carpenter, who fell off one of the bridges spanning the road to cross the digging sites. His death was caused by negligence in securing the bridges and also because of heavy rains making the ground slick and moist. He fell to his death inside the freshly dug Atlantic Avenue tunnel. The second death was caused by a difference of opinion. During the construction process, a British overseer demanded the Irish laborers work Saturdays and Sundays for the same pay and miss church. One laborer, who refused to give up Sunday mass, pulled out a gun and shot the overseer. Supposedly, the crew concealed his body behind a tunnel wall. Presumably his body still lies there today.

Using the cut and cover method, hand tools, and manual labor, the laborers dug up the street for approximately twelve blocks, built a wooden frame, and installed a barrel-vaulted brick roof. The half-mile tunnel accommodates two standard gauge tracks. This engineering feat occurred within seven months in 1844.

The tunnel was used in passenger service for fourteen years, but 1859 it fell into disuse. Vanderbilt had left the railroad for the steamship business in California. Political maneuvering led to trains in Brooklyn being declared a nuisance. The authorities decided that the tunnel should be shut down, filled in, and closed up. A shady operator named Electus Litchfield was awarded the contract to fill in the tunnel. He decided instead to fill in the ends of tunnel, cap up the holes to the street, and coerced some cronies to sign off on his work.

Over the decades, the tunnel became one of many urban legends. People surmised that it contained treasure or, perhaps, John Wilkes Booth's lost diary. River pirates and bootleggers were said to haunt it. No one knew where it was until, in 1981, a young man named Bob Diamond located it.

Of course, many believe the tunnel is haunted. Bob Diamond has seen blue orbs, balls of light, or streaks moving through the tunnel. Most recently, he has reported the sighting of a shadow figure meandering around by the lights only to vanish through the tunnel wall. Perhaps it was that British overseer who wanted the labor force to give up church!

The Brooklyn Historic Railway Association (BHRA) was formed in 1982 to restore the historic tunnel. BHRA successfully filed and received designation for the tunnel on the National Register of Historic Places. Today, you can join a flashlight tour of the world's oldest subway tunnel, which allows you to crawl down through a manhole cover in the middle of busy Atlantic Avenue. A few art events have occurred underground also.

Atlantic Avenue and Court Street
Brooklyn, New York

The Hydesville Rappings

Spiritualism is the belief that the living can communicate with the dead. A medium serves as the intermediary between the individual wishing to converse with the dead and the spirit of the deceased.

In the winter of 1848, the Fox family moved from Rochester to a small cottage among the farm fields of Hydesville, southeast of the city. The Fox family included three young girls Ann, Maggie, and Kate. At first, the family heard a series of knocks and footsteps that they could not account for. They felt vibrations, which affected their chairs and beds.

Highly disturbed by these events, the parents decided that a restless ghost had invaded their home.

The children, however, are reported to have tried communicating with the spirit by snapping their fingers and clapping their hands. Catherine is reported to have spoken aloud while doing so. "Mr. Splitfoot, do as I do," she said and the knocks would then respond in kind! Eventually, the children and their mother could communicate with their spirit, using a series of knocks to spell out the letters of the alphabet. Through this method, the sisters claim to have learned that their spirit was a peddler who had been robbed, murdered, and buried in their house.

The Fox family invited their neighbors to watch this form of communication. The neighbors told other people, and the story spread about the young girls who could communicate with the dead! Ultimately, they dug up the basement but didn't find anything at that time. People began reporting that other spirits were also communicating with the sisters, and that invisible hands were moving objects and lifting tables. Naturally, the fact that these girls could communicate with the spirits of dead fascinated the public.

Spiritualism was born. Soon the girls had a stage act and were paid well to communicate with deceased loved ones. They toured the United States, backed by P.T. Barnum and newspaper editor Horace Greeley.

Within weeks of their success, other "mediums" started to appear. No party or social gathering was complete without a séance in a darkened room with the participants sitting in a circle holding hands. Holding hands prevented anyone from using their hands to produce ghostly phenomenal. Within the darkened room, the medium would speak in different voices and languages; sounds were heard; small physical objects would appear and disappear; furniture would move; and, occasionally, a spirit would "materialize" in a temporary physical form.

Ultimately, many people criticized them, and the Fox Sisters fell upon tough times – personally and professionally. By 1888, the two younger sisters said they simply cracked their toes to mimic rapping sounds from the dead. A year later they recanted their confession, leaving their followers very confused. Many believe that the sisters were a hoax, who made a living out of pretending to talk to the spirits of the dead; others still maintain the truth of the sisters' original story. Today, Spiritualism continues to have hundreds of thousands of followers.

Author's note: In 1904, the gradual disintegration of one of the cellar walls of the Fox house exposed an entire human skeleton. The house was later moved to Lily Dale, the Spiritualist community in New York, where the bones of the "murdered peddler" were displayed for years.

Tree of Hope

At the northern end of Manhattan was Harlem, which remained an urban outpost until the expanding elevated railway system linked it to the rest of the city. Builders saw their opportunity, and white people moved into the many new apartment buildings, brownstones, and tenements in the area. By 1880, black people began living in Harlem, especially in the area around 125th Street. During World War I, the city's industries, which had lost their labor force to the draft, began to recruit black laborers to fill job positions. Masses of blacks began to migrate into Harlem. Many came to flee Southern racism and segregation and to seek better jobs and education for their children; others came from throughout the United States and Jamaica. The latter were often professional, educated, and middle class. By 1920, more than 80,000 blacks lived in Harlem on streets lined with spacious, late-nineteenth century brownstones.

By the 1920s, the emerging new black talent was known as the Negro renaissance. Artists and writers who were active in Harlem in the 1920s helped establish Harlem as the cultural capital of black America. Even more important was the music, specifically Harlem jazz. Jazz made Harlem the place to visit.

In the 1920s, 7th Avenue in Harlem was known as the Boulevard of Dreams. On it stood Harlem's top show business venue, the Lafayette Theatre between 131st and 132nd Streets. Next to it was Connie's Inn, where many came to meet and socialize. The theater was particularly popular with actors.

When the days were warm and the inn became stuffy, people went outside and stood under the shade of a great elm. As the elm tree was in the heart of Harlem's club and theater district, it became a natural place where agents and people in show business would gather. This elm tree became known as a kind of wishing well among the Harlem show people. Young black actors, singers, and dancers would wait in its shade, hoping to be noticed by the talent scouts. They believed that if they touched, stroked, or kissed the bark of the tree, their wishes would come true.

Many entertainment jobs were handed out under the shade of the elm tree, which reinforced its reputation. Soon it was known as The Tree of Hope, symbolizing the promise that Harlem held for so many African Americans and performers such as Ethel Waters, Fletcher Henderson, and Eubie Blake.

In the 1930, plans were made to widen 7th Avenue, and the tree was to be cut down. Many actors, singers, and musicians protested against this action, but the tree, which was in poor condition, had to go. Many people desperate to keep some thing of the tree ripped off pieces of the bark and kept them as good luck charms.

The honorary mayor of Harlem, famed tap dancer and entertainer Bill "Bojangles" Robinson, and a committee went to see Mayor Fiorello La Guardia. He told them that he would plant a new elm tree that wouldn't interfere with anybody walking or riding. A day was set for the tree to be removed and the new tree planted. The day the Tree of Hope was removed, everyone came. One enterprising man began chopping off the branches and selling them as good luck charms. Many people bought them. Mr. Schiffman of Harlem's Apollo Theater is said to have taken a large piece of the tree trunk and placed it in the wings of his theater. On amateur night when the new talents tried to impress the audience, they would touch the tree for good luck.

Then Mayor La Guardia told the crowd that he would set the stump of the old tree in concrete so it would last forever. The trunk was embedded in concrete at the corner of 132nd Street and 7th Avenue. The inscription read:

Tree of Hope
Beloved by the people of Harlem
You asked for a tree of hope
So here it is.
Best wishes.

– Bill Robinson

Unfortunately, that monument became nothing more than a dried-up old stump, surrounded by a small iron fence and a neglected plaque. It certainly didn't resemble a shrine of show business.

In 2004, The Greater Harlem Chamber of Commerce planted a new elm tree near the original site to commemorate Harlem's show business history. They also installed a replica of a long-missing plaque that was commissioned and signed by Bill Robinson to mark the spot of the now-deceased replacement tree that he planted in the median. A second bronze plaque identifies Algernon Miller's colorful, abstract 1972 sculpture, Tree of Hope III.

Adam Powell, Jr. Boulevard
between West 131st and 132nd Streets.

112 Ocean Avenue, Amityville

Some houses inspire stories that appear time and time again. One Dutch Colonial residence, located at 112 Ocean Avenue on the south shore of Long Island in Amityville, has become a well-known haunted house. The events that occurred within its walls have been written about in Jay Anson's 1977 book *The Amityville Horror* and documented in the 1979 film of the same title.

Many believe that paranormal events took place within the house; others insist that it, along with the book and movie, is a hoax. Meanwhile, ghost hunters and tourists are fascinated. To deter their unwanted visitors, residents of the house have altered the house's facade and changed its address to deter unwanted sightseers.

Once upon a time, George and Kathy Lutz and their three small children, Daniel, Christopher, and Melissa (Missy), the children ranging in age from 9 to 5 years old, decided to move into a large Dutch Colonial house in Amityville, New York. It was a very nice home with windows like eyes, a swimming pool, and a boathouse – except that there was a horrific story behind it.

Just a little more than a year before the Lutz family moved in, police had discovered six members of the DeFeo family – father, mother, and four of their five children – shot and killed execution style at the house. The surviving son, Ronald "Butch" DeFeo Jr., was eventually charged and tried for the murder of his family. Currently, he is serving six concurrent life sentences.

Although George and Kathy knew the story of the house, they were determined to live there. It was a much nicer home than their former one. On December 18, 1975, the Lutz family moved into the home, which still contained much of the DeFeo furniture. Although it had only been thirteen months since the DeFeo murders had occurred, the family later claimed at a press conference, "The DeFeo slayings weren't something that would bother us."

On the day they moved in, Father Ray arrived to bless the family's new home. As the Lutzes unloaded their rented moving van, the Catholic priest entered the house and began his ritual blessing alone. He made his way upstairs to the second floor and entered the northeast bedroom, which had been Marc and John DeFeo's room. As he sprinkled holy water around the room and recited a prayer, he heard a loud male voice allegedly say, "Get out!" Although the priest supposedly did not tell the family about the voice, he did warn them about the room, saying, "Don't use it as a bedroom. Don't let anyone sleep in there."

Soon after they arrived, unusual events began to occur. The house was plagued by swarms of flies despite the winter weather. The house had cold spots and odors of perfume and excrement in areas where no wind drafts or piping would explain the source. Green slime oozed from walls in the hall and also from the keyhole of the playroom door in the attic. Kathy hung a twelve-inch crucifix in a closet, which revolved until it was upside down and exuded a sour smell.

Kathy had vivid nightmares about the murder and would feel like an unseen force was embracing her. While in bed, Kathy received red welts on her chest caused by an unseen force and was levitated two feet off the bed. She also discovered a small, hidden room painted red behind shelving in the basement. The five-foot by four-foot room did not appear in the blueprints of the house. The room came to be known as "The Red Room." The Lutz' dog, Harry, refused to go near the room, cringing as if he sensed something evil.

George had problems sleeping. He would hear the front door slamming, but when he raced downstairs he would find the dog sleeping soundly at the front door. Nobody else heard it. Sometimes George would hear what was described as a "German marching band tuning up" or what sounded like a clock radio playing not quite on frequency. When he went downstairs, the noise would stop. George tripped over an ornamental four-foot high china lion in the living room and was left with bite marks on one of his ankles. One day he saw Kathy transformed into an old woman of ninety, "the hair wild, a shocking white, the face a mass of wrinkles and ugly lines, and saliva dripping from the toothless mouth." He was obsessed with the need to check on things in the boathouse.

The family began to hear strange noises every night. George would rush to find where they were coming from. It sounded like they came from the attic but when he got there, he would hear new sounds coming from the first floor. When he reached the living room, he found the furniture had been moved.

As a family, they decide not to let the house scare them. They had a dinner party for their neighbors. While they were there, they too heard the noises. The Lutzes and the guests investigated each room trying to find the source of the noises. Once the terrified guests left, they even tried asking the spirits to leave. "Please go back to where you came from."

"Please leave," sobbed Kathy.

"I beg of you," said George.

The evil atmosphere persisted. Kathy would often feel someone behind her when she was in the kitchen. They all saw glowing eyes looking in the windows. Shadows filled the house.

Then their five-year-old daughter, Missy, announced that she had a new friend. Friends were nice, thought Kathy, but then she found out that this friend wasn't imaginary.

"Who is Jodie, Missy?"

"He's my friend. He can change his shape. He says I'm going to live in this house forever."

Kathy discovered that Jodie was a demonic pig-like creature with glowing red eyes. While checking the boathouse one night, George saw a pair of red eyes looking at him from Missy's bedroom window. When he went upstairs to her room, there was nothing to be found. George discovered hoof prints outside. The family fought back. Kathy threw a chair at one set of eyes, but the house uttered a horrific scream.

The book reported that the malevolent forces caused significant property damage to the house, such as the screen door being ripped off its hinges, windows being smashed, banisters being torn from their fittings, damage to the garage door, and water damage from hurricane-force winds, which local meteorological stations had no record of.

After deciding that something was wrong with their house that they could not explain rationally, George and Kathy Lutz carried out a blessing of their own on January 8, 1976. George held a silver crucifix while they both recited the Lord's Prayer. When in the living room, George allegedly heard a chorus of voices shouting at them, "Will you stop?" By mid-January 1976, and after another attempt at a house blessing by George and Kathy, they experienced what would turn out to be their final night in the house. The Lutzes refused to describe the events that occurred on this occasion, describing them as "too frightening."

The terrorized family rushed to leave the house. The walls of the house appeared to be moving around them. They heard groaning noises. As they left the house, George met a ghost. Days later, paranormal investigators came to the house and sensed a horrible presence in the home.

Many years have passed, but the Lutzes continue to stick to their story.

Today, the house has been renovated extensively. A sunroom has been added on the back of the house to give it a more symmetrical look, and the driveway has been repaved. These are just some of the extensive (and expensive) changes the owner has incurred. Why? Because the new owners love the property!

112 Ocean Avenue
Amityville, New York

The Ghosts of Ground Zero

Almost everyone knows where he or she was on that beautiful fall day. It was the kind of day that made New Yorkers fall in love with the city again. But then at 8:45 a.m., American Airlines Flight 11 smashed into the World Trade Center Number One, the North Tower, at the 94th floor – more than 1,000 feet above ground. Seventeen minutes later, at 9:03, United Airlines Flight 175 hit the South Tower, World Trade Center Two. The South Tower collapsed at 9:59 a.m., and the North Tower followed at 10:28 a.m.

In total, 2,700 vertical feet of building, containing nearly 10 million square feet of floor space, was reduced to a tangled heap less than 200 feet thick, encompassing more than 34 acres. Four hundred million pounds of steel columns, trusses, and reinforcing bars from the two towers were twisted into scrap. Six hundred thousand square feet of thick window glass were splintered (Stout, Vitchers, Gray, p. 21)

Inside and near the towers, 2,753 people were killed, including all 157 passengers and crew aboard the two aircraft. Falling rubble from the collapsing towers and subsequent fires severely damaged or destroyed more than a dozen other adjacent and nearby structures. In the twenty-four hours following the attacks, thousands of New Yorkers trudged northwards away from horror and chaos. Thousands of other rescue workers pushed toward the site.

Life changed forever on the morning of 9/11. Perhaps for New Yorkers it changed the most as choking black smoke smothered downtown Manhattan on that beautiful fall day. Soon flames could be seen, and debris, paper, and worse began to rain on to the plaza.

The ghosts will always be there as proven on a May morning in 2009 when New Yorkers all across downtown Manhattan – where the World Trade Center once stood – watched in horror as a massive aircraft, trailed closely by an F-16 fighter jet, banked and roared low near the city, in a frightening echo of the events of September 11, 2001. Fearing the worst, thousands of people streamed out of the skyscrapers and into the streets. Some buildings ordered evacuations. Many people took shelter in shops to call loved ones on their cell phones.

The Chapel

Near the site of the World Trade Center stands St. Paul's Chapel, a tiny eighteenth-century Episcopal church. Opened in 1766 at Broadway and Fulton Streets as part of the vast Trinity Church Wall Street parish, it is the oldest public building in Manhattan in continuous use. George Washington once worshipped there. The chapel has a history of being a relief center during disaster. In September 1776, it had escaped a major fire, which destroyed nearly a third of the city's housing and became a refuge for hundreds of needy New Yorkers at that time.

Although the chapel withstood the collapse of the buildings, the building and churchyard were covered in inches of dust from the Twin Towers' collapse. After engineers inspected the Church building and pronounced it fit for occupancy, the digging out began. The chapel staff used candles and flashlights until city workers set up crude lamps. Meanwhile, firemen, policemen, ironworkers, carpenters, office workers, doctors, and dogs were searching for survivors, going deep into the subterranean levels, pouring over the rubble, removing bodies and body parts. Following their shifts, they came to the Chapel to eat and rest.

By September 15, the chapel and its volunteers were feeding hundreds of exhausted and hungry relief workers grilled hamburgers, giving them new socks and gloves, and treating stiff muscles and burned feet. By October 1, St. Paul's ministry began to evolve into a well-organized operation for the workers at Ground Zero. Hundreds of volunteers worked twelve-hour shifts, twenty-four hours a day, tending to the physical, emotional, and spiritual needs of the rescue, construction, and security workers on the site. Some of the city's best kitchens donated gourmet fare for the workers. St. Paul's assigned tasks to volunteers from across the country and organized chaplains on a round-the-clock schedule. Long tables were piled high with fresh fruit, and boxes overflowed with candy, cookies, chips, power bars, gum, and cigarettes. Cards, notes, banners, and teddy bears began to arrive from around the world, and volunteers displayed them throughout the Chapel. The Vienna Boys' Choir sang at the Chapel, and worldwide visitors to Ground Zero stopped at St. Paul's as part of their traditional Christmas visit to New York. More than 5,000 people used their special gifts to transform St. Paul's into a place of rest and refuge.

Today, you can visit the ghosts of that effort. You can honor those who labored nine long months to recover the human remains. You can sit on the pews, which were beds for the rescue workers. You can see artifacts left behind by the doctors, musicians, lawyers, and all those many others who came to pour coffee, rub tired feet, serve meals, and listen to the agonies of the rescue workers as they located and removed human remains from Ground Zero. Day after day, they sifted through the debris from the smoldering pit of Ground Zero across the street. Now years later, we can grab our tissues and mourn for those who have been lost and pay tribute to those who provided light during weeks of darkness.

209 Broadway at Fulton Street
Lower Manhattan, New York

Conclusion

"One belongs to New York instantly, one belongs to it as much in five minutes as in five years."

– Thomas Wolfe

Most of us don't think of New York as a state with ghosts, legends, or even an occasional monster. When we think about New York State, we think about Niagara Falls, the City that never sleeps, the Catskills, the Adirondacks, or the Finger Lakes. If we are into history, we think of the Dutch, the Battle of Saratoga, Erie Canal, the Draft Riots of 1863, or September 11.

Some say in 1784, five years before George Washington was inaugurated as the first president of the United States in New York City, he envisioned New York as the "seat of empire," thus giving rise to its nickname – the Empire State. Others say that nineteenth century New York earned that name because of its great wealth and natural resources. Certainly, the state is a gateway for immigration to the United States and a world-renowned financial, cultural, transportation, and manufacturing center.

But New York State is also a magnet for the supernatural. Its ghosts have no compunction about night or day. They come and go as they wish. The voices of its past can still be heard reliving those frightful moments that sealed their fate. The wind carries them in between the skyscrapers, over the lakes, and up through the hills. Some say it is just an old draft, a curtain blowing in the wind, a strange sound in the dark of the cellar, or a shadow hovering in the drafty hall. If you listen carefully, however, to those wheezy inhales and exhales, the rustling of the leaves, or the stealthy footsteps, you will hear voices from the past, saying, "Listen, remember us." Some of us, if we turn quickly enough, might even see them. For we are never alone; they are there. They are our roots; they are our future.

When the clock nears midnight on December 31, people throughout the world turn to the neon-lit crowds and dynamic world of Times Square. Times Square, sometimes known as the "Crossroads of the World," has achieved the status of an iconic world landmark and has become a symbol of its city. *Courtesy of D. Peter Lund*

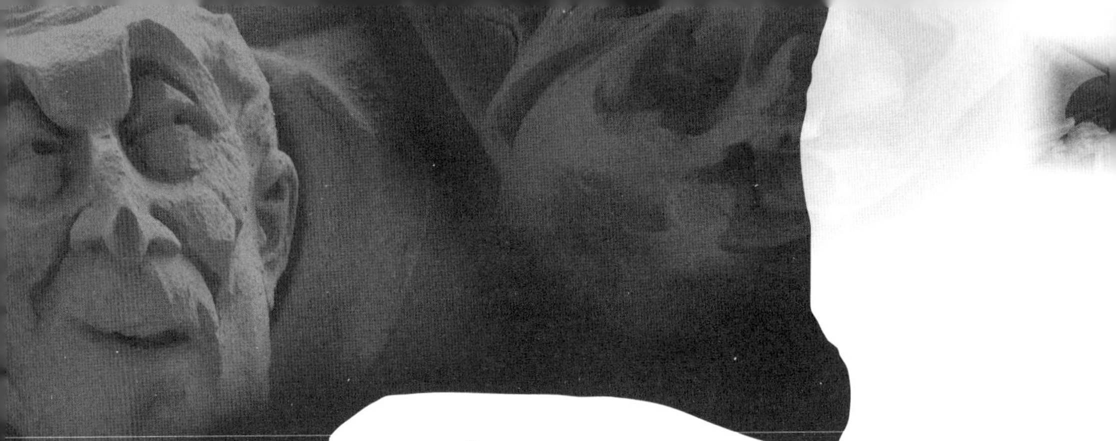

Bibliography

Print Publications

Barr, Lockwood. *A Brief, But Most Complete & True Account of the Settlement of the Ancient Town of Pelham Westchester County, State of New York Known One Time Well & Favourably as The Lordshipp & Manour of Pelham Also the Story of the Three Modern Villages Called the Pelhams*, pp. 135-36 (The Dietz Press 1946).

Bordman, Gerald and Thomas S. Hischak. "Belasco Theatre." *The Oxford Companion to American Theatre*. New York, New York. Oxford University Press. 2004.

Caldwell, Mark. *New York, New York.* New York, New York: Scribner, 2005.

Casey, Tom. "Tales of Headless Indians at the Haunted Cedar Knoll." *Bronx Times Reporter.* May 9, 2002.

Carmer, Carl. *The Screaming Ghost and Other Stories.*

—, New York, New York: Alfred A. Knopf. 1956.

Freedgood, Seymour. *The Gateway States*. New York, New York: Time Incorporated. 1967.

Gordon, Hanford Lennox. *Pauline And Other Poems*. New York, New York: G.P. Putnam, 1898.

Guerber, Helene A. *The Story of the Thirteen Colonies.* Stanford University Libraries.

Hale, Sally. "The Unfinished Love Story of the Thousand Islands." In *All Points North*, Fall 2006.

Hamilton, Chris. "Man calls for law to protect Bigfoot." *Capital News 9*.

Hudson, Mike. " Suicide Season." *Niagara Falls.* May 27, 2008.

Jagendorf, M. A. *The Ghost of Peg-Leg Peter*. New York, New York: Vanguard Press.

James, Alexa. "Ghost Stories Fly at West Point." *Times Herald-Record.* May 9, 2009.

Jones, Louis Clark, *Things That Go Bump in The Night.* New York, New York, New York: Hill and Wang. 1959.
Klein, Milton (Ed.) *The Empire State*. Ithaca, New York: Cornell University Press 2001.
McGrath, Ben. "Ectoplasm." *The New Yorker,* April 15, 2009.
Morrison, William. *Broadway Theatres.* Mineola, New York: Dover Publications, Inc. 1999.
Myers, Arthur. *The Ghostly Register.* Chicago, Illinois: James Peter Associates, 1986.
New York Times. "5,000,000 Loss in Capitol Fire." March 30, 1911.
New York Times. "George Boldt Dies." December 6, 1916, p. 9.
New York Post. "Friendly Ghosts Haunt Hotel." October 28, 2006.
Paumgarten Nick. "A Broadway Haunt. " *The New Yorker*, February 25, 2009.
Pitkin, David J. *Ghosts of the Northeast*. Salem, New York: Aurora Publications. 2002.
Revai, Cheri, *Haunted New York.* New York, New York: Stackpole Books. 1963.
Schoener, Allon. *New York.* New York, New York: W.W. Norton & Company. 1998.
Stout, Glenn, Vitchers, Charles, and Gray, Robert. *Nine Months at Ground Zero.* New York City, New York: Scribner 2006.
Time Magazine. "Phantom of the Point." Monday, Dec. 04, 1972.
Vernon, Alex. "Ghost Stories." *American Heritage Magazine.* October 2002.
Widdicombe, Lizzie, "Skunked," *The New Yorker*. August 27, 2007.
Wonderley, Anthony. *Oneida Iroquois Folklore, Myth, and History.* Syracuse. New York: Syracuse University Press. 2004.

Internet

BFRO Geographical Database of Bigfoot Sightings & Reports
Chorvinsky, Mark. NESSIE and Other Lake Monsters. Strangemag.com.
Fontenot, Robert "Did John Lennon have any signs of his impending death?" About.com: Oldies Music. December 28, 1980.
LakeChamplainAngler.net. "Champ. The Lake Champlain Monster."
Museum of Unnatural History. "Champ of Lake Champlain."
Oneida Indian Nation.com. "The Polly Cooper Shawl at the Shako:wi Cultural Center." Aug 15, 2008.
The Press Republican. "Does BigFoot roam the North Country?" April 18, 2009.

Index